CHAPTER 1: INTRODUCTION TO BLENDER

In the introductory phase of exploring Blender, we begin with a meticulous examination of its interface, which serves as the central hub for all creative endeavors within this 3D animation software. The interface is thoughtfully designed to accommodate the diverse needs of 3D artists, from modeling and texturing to rendering and animation. Understanding the layout and functionality of this interface is paramount to effectively utilizing Blender's capabilities.

Upon launching Blender, you are greeted with a default workspace that features several distinct areas, each playing a crucial role in the 3D creation process. The initial view is dominated by the 3D Viewport, which occupies the central portion of the interface. This is where the primary interactions with the 3D model occur. The Viewport allows for the manipulation and visualization of 3D objects from various angles. Tools for navigation and transformation are accessible here, enabling users to rotate, pan, and zoom into their work. Mastery of these navigation controls is essential for precise modeling and animation tasks.

To the left of the 3D Viewport lies the Tool Shelf, an area that provides quick access to commonly used tools and functions. This shelf can be customized to display tools specific to the current task, whether it be mesh editing, sculpting, or texture painting. Understanding how to efficiently use and customize this shelf can significantly enhance productivity by reducing the need to frequently access menus.

Adjacent to the Tool Shelf is the Properties Editor, located on the right side of the interface. This editor is a vital component for modifying the attributes and settings of objects within your project. It is divided into several tabs, each corresponding to different categories such as Render Settings, Material Properties, Modifiers, and Object Data. Each tab provides a range of options that allow for detailed adjustments and fine-tuning of various elements within the project. For instance, the Material Properties tab is where users can define the appearance of objects through shaders and textures, while the Modifiers tab allows for the application of procedural transformations to models.

Below the 3D Viewport and Properties Editor, the Timeline and Dope Sheet editors are positioned. These tools are crucial for animation tasks. The Timeline provides a visual representation of the animation sequence and keyframes, allowing users to control the timing and sequence of animations. The Dope Sheet, on the other hand, offers a more detailed view of keyframe data, enabling precise adjustments to animation curves and timings. Familiarity with these tools is essential for creating smooth and coherent animations.

Navigating through Blender's interface also involves an understanding of the Outliner, typically located in a panel on the right or the top-right section of the workspace. The Outliner is a hierarchical view of all objects within the scene, providing an organized list of elements such as meshes, cameras, lights, and more. It is an indispensable tool for managing and selecting objects, especially in complex scenes with numerous elements. Users can utilize the Outliner to quickly locate and hide or show objects, making scene management more efficient.

As you begin a new project in Blender, the process typically starts with creating a new file, which can be done via the File menu. Once a new project is initiated, you are presented with a default scene containing a basic set of objects, including a cube, a camera, and a light source. This default setup is designed to help users quickly get started with their projects without having to set up a scene from scratch. To begin modeling, you can start by selecting the default cube or adding new objects using the Add menu in the 3D Viewport. Objects can be added as meshes, curves, or surfaces, among other types, each serving different purposes within the modeling process.

The initial step in modeling involves understanding the various modes available in Blender, such as Object Mode and Edit Mode. Object Mode is used for manipulating entire objects, including moving, scaling, and rotating. Edit Mode, on the other hand, allows for more granular control, enabling users to edit the individual components of a mesh, such as vertices, edges, and faces. Switching between these modes is achieved through the interaction menu or keyboard shortcuts, and mastering these modes is critical for effective modeling.

Basic operations in modeling include manipulating the mesh's geometry through tools such as Extrude, Scale, and Rotate. The Extrude tool is used to extend geometry from selected faces, which is fundamental for building complex shapes from simple forms. The Scale tool adjusts the size of selected components, while the Rotate tool changes their orientation. These tools, combined with the ability to navigate and view the model from different angles, form the backbone of 3D modeling in Blender.

In addition to the core tools, Blender also incorporates a range of modifiers that can be applied to objects to achieve various effects and transformations non-destructively. Modifiers such as Subdivision Surface and Mirror can significantly streamline the modeling process by allowing users to refine and duplicate their work with minimal manual adjustments. Understanding how to use these modifiers effectively can enhance both the quality and efficiency of your 3D models.

The introduction to Blender's interface and tools lays the groundwork for more advanced topics. By familiarizing yourself with the workspace layout, navigation techniques, and basic modeling concepts, you establish a solid foundation for exploring the broader range of features and functionalities that Blender offers. As you become more comfortable with these fundamental elements, you will be well-prepared to delve into more complex aspects of 3D animation and rendering.

As we delve further into the basics of Blender, it's essential to become acquainted with the core concepts of 3D modeling. The process of 3D modeling in Blender begins with the creation and manipulation of basic geometric shapes, often referred to as primitives. These shapes include cubes, spheres, cylinders, and cones, which serve as the building blocks for more complex structures. Understanding how to effectively use these primitives is fundamental to creating and refining 3D models.

To create a new object, one begins by selecting the "Add" menu, accessible via a right-click within the 3D Viewport. This menu offers a variety of primitives that can be added to the scene. Upon adding a primitive, it appears in the center of the Viewport, and its position, scale, and orientation can be adjusted using the transformation tools. These tools include Move, Rotate, and Scale, which are accessible from the toolbar or via shortcut keys. Mastering these tools is crucial for shaping and positioning objects accurately within the 3D space.

Once a primitive is added, it can be further modified through Edit Mode. Switching to Edit Mode allows for more granular control over the object's geometry. In Edit Mode, the object's vertices, edges, and faces become selectable, enabling detailed manipulation. This mode is essential for tasks such as extruding new geometry, subdividing faces, and merging vertices. Each of these operations is performed through specific tools and commands that alter the mesh structure. For instance, the Extrude tool extends geometry from selected faces, which is useful for adding detail to a model.

The concept of Modifiers also plays a significant role in 3D modeling within Blender. Modifiers are non-destructive operations that can be applied to objects to alter their appearance or behavior without permanently changing the original mesh. Common modifiers include the Subdivision Surface modifier, which smooths out geometry by increasing its polygon count, and the Boolean modifier, which allows for the combination or subtraction of objects to create complex shapes. Modifiers are managed through the Modifiers tab in the Properties Editor, where they can be added, adjusted, or removed as needed.

Understanding the principles of UV Mapping is another critical aspect of 3D modeling. UV Mapping involves unwrapping a 3D model into a 2D plane to apply textures accurately. This process ensures that textures are applied in a way that aligns with the model's surface. Blender offers several unwrapping methods, such as Smart UV Project and Unwrap, which can be selected based on the complexity and requirements of the model. Once the model is unwrapped, textures can be painted or applied using image files. The UV/Image Editor provides a visual representation of the UV layout and allows for texture adjustments.

In addition to modeling, Blender's sculpting tools provide an alternative approach to creating and refining 3D models. Sculpting is akin to working with digital clay, allowing for more organic and fluid modifications. Blender's sculpting workspace includes a variety of brushes and tools that can be used to push, pull, smooth, and refine the model's surface. This method is particularly useful for creating detailed characters and complex organic shapes. The Dynamic Topology feature in sculpting allows for real-time mesh refinement, adding detail as needed without predefined resolution limits.

As you become more comfortable with Blender's basic modeling and sculpting tools, the next step is to familiarize yourself with the concept of Materials and Shaders. Materials define the visual properties of an object, such as its color, texture, and reflectivity. Blender utilizes a node-based system for creating and managing materials, which provides a powerful and flexible way to achieve various visual effects. The Shader Editor is where materials are created and modified using nodes, which represent different properties and functions. For instance, the Principled BSDF shader node is a versatile option that can simulate a wide range of materials from metals to plastics.

The integration of Lighting and Camera setup is also vital for creating realistic and visually appealing renders. Proper lighting enhances the model's appearance and helps to set the desired mood. Blender offers several types of lights, including Point, Sun, Spot, and Area lights, each with distinct characteristics and uses. The placement and configuration of these lights can significantly impact the final render. Similarly, the Camera object determines the perspective from which the scene is viewed and rendered. Adjusting the camera's focal length, depth of field, and position is crucial for achieving the desired composition and visual effect in the final output.

Lastly, the process of rendering is the culmination of all the modeling, texturing, and lighting work. Blender's rendering engines, Eevee and Cycles, offer different approaches to generating final images or animations. Eevee is a real-time render engine that provides quick feedback and is suitable for interactive previews, while Cycles is a ray-tracing engine known for its high-quality results and realistic light simulation. The Render Settings tab in the Properties Editor allows for the configuration of render parameters, such as resolution, output format, and sampling rates.

With these foundational tools and concepts, you are well-prepared to embark on more complex and creative projects within Blender. The skills and knowledge acquired at this stage will serve as a strong base for exploring advanced features and techniques in subsequent stages of your 3D animation journey.

When exploring the intricacies of UV Mapping within Blender, it is crucial to understand how this process enables the application of textures onto 3D models. UV Mapping involves flattening a 3D model's surface onto a 2D plane, creating a UV map. This map is essential for accurately applying textures and ensuring they align correctly with the model's geometry.

To begin UV Mapping, one first enters Edit Mode and selects the geometry to be unwrapped. Blender provides several unwrapping methods, such as Smart UV Project, which automatically calculates the UV coordinates based on the model's geometry, and Unwrap, which allows for more manual control by specifying seams. Seams are essentially edges where the 3D model is "cut" to lay it flat. Placing seams strategically helps minimize texture distortion and ensures that the final UV map appears as intended.

After unwrapping, the UV map can be viewed and edited in the UV Editor, which displays the 2D representation of the model's surface. In the UV Editor, you can adjust the UV islands—regions of the UV map that correspond to different parts of the 3D model. These adjustments involve scaling, rotating, and moving UV islands to optimize texture placement and reduce stretching. Ensuring that UV islands are properly arranged and spaced is essential for maintaining texture quality and consistency.

Next, let's discuss the rendering process, which transforms your 3D model into a final image or animation. Rendering in Blender is controlled through the Render Settings found in the Properties Editor. These settings determine various aspects of how the final output will be generated, including resolution, sampling quality, and output format. Two primary rendering engines are available: Cycles and Eevee. Cycles is a path-tracing renderer that offers high realism by simulating light interactions more accurately, while Eevee is a real-time renderer that provides faster results with more limited realism. The choice between these engines depends on the balance between render quality and speed required for your project.

Rendering involves several critical steps. First, you set up your scene by positioning lights and cameras. Proper lighting is essential for highlighting details and creating the desired mood. Blender provides various light sources, such as point lights, sun lights, and area lights, each offering different properties and effects. Cameras are placed in the scene to frame the view of the model, and their settings, such as focal length and depth of field, are adjusted to achieve the desired composition.

Once the scene is set, you configure the render settings, including choosing the render engine and specifying the output dimensions. For high-quality renders, increasing the Sampling rate in Cycles improves image fidelity by reducing noise. However, higher sampling rates also increase render times. In Eevee, settings such as Screen Space Reflections and Ambient Occlusion can be adjusted to enhance visual effects while maintaining real-time performance.

Finally, rendering is initiated through the Render menu. Blender processes the scene based on the configured settings and generates the final image or animation sequence. The resulting render can be saved in various formats, such as PNG for still images or MP4 for animations. Reviewing the final output often involves analyzing the quality and making adjustments to lighting, materials, or render settings as needed.

Understanding these foundational aspects of Blender equips you with the essential tools and knowledge to start creating your own 3D models and animations. The journey from navigating the interface and modeling basics to UV Mapping and rendering forms the bedrock of more advanced techniques and projects. As you become more familiar with these concepts, you will be better prepared to tackle more complex tasks and refine your skills in 3D creation. The knowledge acquired here will serve as a solid foundation for exploring more intricate features and workflows within Blender in the future.

CHAPTER 2:
BASIC MODELING
TECHNIQUES

In this exploration of basic modeling techniques, we delve into the essential practices required to construct and refine geometric shapes within Blender. The foundation of 3D modeling in Blender involves manipulating vertices, edges, and faces—each fundamental to shaping objects and defining their structure. This section will equip you with a comprehensive understanding of these core elements and the tools used to modify them, setting the stage for more advanced modeling endeavors.

The journey begins with an introduction to Edit Mode, which is indispensable for fine-tuning geometric details. Transitioning from Object Mode to Edit Mode allows for precise control over a model's mesh. In Edit Mode, the mesh is divided into its basic components: vertices (points in 3D space), edges (lines connecting vertices), and faces (surfaces enclosed by edges). Mastery of these components is crucial for effective modeling.

One of the primary tools in Edit Mode is the Selection Tool, which enables users to select vertices, edges, or faces for modification. Using the selection tools efficiently is key to managing complex models. The Box Select tool allows for selecting multiple components within a defined rectangular area, while the Circle Select tool provides a more freeform selection within a circular region. Once selected, vertices, edges, or faces can be manipulated using various transformation tools.

The Grab/Move tool is used to reposition selected components. By clicking and dragging, you can move these elements along the X, Y, and Z axes, altering the model's shape and structure. Precision in moving components is often necessary for aligning parts of a model or achieving specific design objectives.

The Rotate tool, accessible via the shortcut key 'R', allows for the rotation of selected components around a pivot point. This tool is essential for adjusting the orientation of elements, whether aligning edges or creating intricate details. Understanding the different rotation options, such as rotating around specific axes or using the 3D manipulator widget, enhances control over the modeling process.

The Scale tool adjusts the size of selected components. By scaling vertices, edges, or faces, you can modify the proportions of your model, making it larger or smaller as needed. Scaling can be uniform, affecting all dimensions equally, or constrained to specific axes, providing control over individual dimensions.

Another fundamental technique in modeling is Extrusion, which involves extending geometry from a selected face or edge. This operation is particularly useful for adding depth or complexity to a model. By selecting a face and using the Extrude tool, you create new geometry that extends outward from the selected face, thereby increasing the model's complexity. The extruded geometry can then be further manipulated with other tools to achieve the desired shape.

Subdivision is a technique used to increase the polygon count of a model, thereby smoothing out its surfaces. The Subdivision Surface modifier, when applied to a model, divides its faces into smaller polygons, resulting in a smoother appearance. This process is particularly useful for creating organic shapes or highly detailed models. The level of subdivision can be adjusted to balance between detail and computational efficiency.

When constructing models, it is often necessary to Merge vertices, which combines two or more vertices into a single point. This operation is useful for eliminating unwanted geometry and ensuring that the model has a clean, continuous surface. The Merge at Center function merges selected vertices at the geometric center of their selection, while Merge at First and Merge at Last functions consolidate vertices based on their positional order.

The Knife Tool allows for precise cutting of geometry, enabling the creation of new edges and vertices within an existing mesh. By drawing cuts across a model's surface, you can define additional detail or partition areas of the mesh for further modification. The Knife Tool offers various modes and constraints, such as snapping to vertices or edges, which aids in accurate cutting.

In addition to these tools and techniques, Blender provides several Mesh Editing Operations that are pivotal in modeling. Operations like Beveling edges or vertices can add complexity and detail to your model by creating chamfered edges or rounded corners. The Inset Faces operation allows for the creation of new geometry within a face, which can be used to add details such as panels or inset features.

Finally, it is important to familiarize yourself with Topology concepts. Good topology ensures that your model has a clean, efficient mesh structure, which is crucial for both rendering and animation. Proper topology involves using quads (four-sided polygons) rather than triangles or n-gons (polygons with more than four sides), as quads tend to deform more predictably during animation.

As you progress in your modeling skills, these basic techniques will serve as the building blocks for creating increasingly complex and detailed 3D models. Mastery of vertices, edges, faces, and the various tools available in Blender will provide a solid foundation for further exploration into more advanced modeling techniques and practices.

An additional fundamental technique in 3D modeling is the Extrude tool, which is pivotal for extending geometry and adding new detail to your model. When in Edit Mode, selecting faces or edges and then using the Extrude tool allows you to pull out new geometry from the selected components. This tool is invaluable for creating complex shapes and forms by adding new faces and manipulating existing ones. The extruded geometry can be adjusted in various ways—moving it along different axes, scaling it, or rotating it to achieve the desired shape. This technique is often used in architectural modeling, character design, and any scenario where extending geometry is necessary to build up a model's structure.

Another crucial modeling operation is Subdividing. The Subdivide tool increases the number of polygons in a selected face or edge, thereby adding detail and allowing for smoother and more complex shapes. This technique is particularly useful when refining a model to ensure smooth surfaces or when preparing a model for animation. The level of subdivision can be controlled, allowing for a balance between detail and performance. Subdivision is typically applied to larger faces or areas where additional detail is required, and it can be adjusted dynamically to meet the needs of the model.

To further refine your models, the Merge tool comes into play. Merging vertices allows you to combine multiple vertices into a single point, which can be essential for cleaning up a model or ensuring that geometry aligns correctly. This tool is particularly useful when dealing with overlapping vertices or when simplifying the mesh to reduce complexity. The Merge tool can be used to merge vertices by distance or by specifying exact coordinates, ensuring precise control over the resulting geometry.

Edge Loop and Ring Tools are additional techniques that enhance the modeling workflow. The Edge Loop tool allows you to select a continuous loop of edges around a model, which is useful for adding new detail or for adjusting the flow of the geometry. Similarly, the Edge Ring tool selects a continuous ring of edges, which can be used for similar purposes. Both tools facilitate the process of adding or modifying edge loops around the model, allowing for more controlled and refined adjustments.

Beveling is another important technique for refining edges and adding detail to a model. The Bevel tool allows you to create a chamfered edge by splitting an edge into multiple segments and then adjusting their positions. This technique is used to soften hard edges or to add detail to corners and intersections. By adjusting the width and segments of the bevel, you can control the amount of detail and smoothness applied to the edges of your model.

When working on a model, it's also important to be familiar with Sculpting Tools. Sculpting in Blender allows for a more organic approach to modeling, where you can manipulate the mesh with brush-like tools to create detailed and complex forms. Sculpting is often used in character modeling or in scenarios where traditional polygonal modeling is less efficient. The sculpting brushes, such as Draw, Smooth, Clay, and Inflate, each offer different ways to modify the mesh, enabling the creation of intricate details and textures.

The Modifiers panel also plays a significant role in basic modeling techniques. Modifiers are non-destructive operations that can be applied to the model to alter its appearance or behavior. For example, the Mirror modifier allows you to create symmetrical models by applying transformations to only one half of the model, with the other half being automatically updated. This is particularly useful for modeling symmetrical objects, such as characters or architectural elements. Other modifiers, such as the Subdivision Surface modifier, smooth out the geometry by adding additional subdivisions, thereby creating a more polished appearance.

Understanding Normals is crucial for ensuring proper shading and rendering of your model. Normals are vectors perpendicular to the faces of the model and determine how light interacts with the surface. Ensuring that normals are correctly oriented is important for achieving accurate lighting and shading effects. In Blender, you can recalculate or flip normals to correct any issues with face orientation, which helps prevent visual artifacts and ensures a smooth appearance in the final render.

As you progress in mastering these basic modeling techniques, it's essential to continually practice and experiment with different tools and methods. Each technique serves a specific purpose and, when combined effectively, can lead to the creation of sophisticated and detailed 3D models. Through consistent application of these fundamental techniques, you will build a strong foundation for more advanced modeling practices and achieve proficiency in creating and refining 3D objects within Blender.

The Bevel tool is particularly effective for creating smooth transitions between edges, enhancing the realism of your models. By selecting an edge or a set of edges and applying the Bevel tool, you can create a chamfered edge by dividing the selected edge into multiple segments. This process introduces additional geometry, which can be adjusted to control the width and depth of the bevel. Beveling not only adds visual interest but also improves the appearance of models by preventing the overly sharp edges that can appear in realistic rendering scenarios.

In addition to these tools, the Knife tool allows for precise cutting and detailing of your model's mesh. By entering Knife Tool mode, you can draw cuts directly onto your model, creating new edges and vertices where needed. This tool is invaluable for adding intricate details and refining the geometry of your model. The Knife tool operates in various modes, such as Freehand and Exact, providing flexibility depending on the level of precision required. After making a cut, vertices and edges can be further manipulated using the other transformation tools to integrate the new geometry seamlessly into your model.

The Sculpting mode within Blender offers an alternative approach to modeling, providing a more intuitive and artistic way to shape and detail your models. Sculpting allows for dynamic interaction with the model, using brushes to push, pull, smooth, and otherwise manipulate the surface. This method is particularly useful for organic shapes and detailed textures, where traditional polygonal modeling might be cumbersome. Various brushes and settings are available to tailor the sculpting process to specific needs, such as adding fine details or smoothing out rough areas. Sculpting is often used in conjunction with retopology techniques to create a clean, animation-ready mesh.

Modifiers in Blender further enhance the modeling process by allowing non-destructive changes to your model. For example, the Subdivision Surface modifier can be applied to increase the mesh's polygon count, smoothing out surfaces and adding detail without altering the base geometry. The Mirror modifier is useful for creating symmetrical models, automatically mirroring changes made to one half of the model to the other. These modifiers can be adjusted and removed at any time, offering flexibility during the modeling process.

Understanding Normals is also crucial for effective modeling and rendering. Normals are vectors that define the direction a face is pointing, and they affect how light interacts with the surface. Incorrectly oriented normals can lead to rendering issues, such as visible seams or shading artifacts. In Blender, normals can be recalculated and adjusted to ensure proper shading and light interaction. The Recalculate Normals function, found in the Mesh menu, automatically corrects the orientation of normals, while manual adjustments can be made using the Normals submenu for more control.

Finally, it's important to emphasize the significance of Mesh Cleanup and Optimization. As models become more complex, they may accumulate unnecessary geometry or overlapping vertices that can impact performance and rendering quality. Blender provides several tools for cleaning up and optimizing meshes, such as the Merge by Distance function, which consolidates vertices that are within a specified distance of each other. Additionally, the Remove Doubles feature can eliminate duplicate vertices, streamlining the mesh and improving efficiency. Regular cleanup and optimization are essential practices to maintain the integrity and performance of your models, ensuring they are ready for further refinement and eventual use in animations or games.

CHAPTER 3: ADVANCED MODELING

In this exploration of advanced modeling techniques, we will expand upon foundational skills to delve into more sophisticated methods and tools available within Blender. This section will cover advanced sculpting techniques, the application of various modifiers, and strategies for managing complex meshes. Our goal is to equip you with the knowledge required to create intricate models and optimize them for practical use, including animation.

Sculpting represents a significant departure from traditional polygonal modeling, offering a more intuitive and flexible approach to creating detailed and organic shapes. To begin sculpting, switch to Sculpt Mode within Blender, which provides access to a suite of sculpting brushes and tools. The primary advantage of sculpting is its ability to manipulate the mesh in a way that feels more akin to working with physical clay. Brushes like the Draw, Clay, Smooth, and Inflate tools allow you to add, remove, and refine surface details with a high degree of control.

The Dynamic Topology feature enhances the sculpting process by dynamically adjusting the mesh's resolution as you sculpt. This means that as you add detail to specific areas, Blender automatically increases the mesh density in those regions while maintaining a lower density elsewhere. This feature is particularly useful for creating highly detailed models without unnecessarily increasing the overall polygon count. Dynamic Topology allows for more efficient sculpting workflows by reducing the need for pre-planning mesh density and manually subdividing the model.

In addition to sculpting, Blender's Modifiers play a crucial role in advanced modeling. Modifiers are non-destructive tools that alter the geometry of your model without permanently changing its base structure. The Subdivision Surface modifier, for example, smooths out your model by adding additional polygonal detail. This is particularly useful for achieving a high level of detail in organic shapes or when preparing models for high-resolution renders. The modifier's settings allow you to adjust the number of subdivisions, balancing between detail and performance.

The Boolean modifier is another powerful tool for advanced modeling, enabling the combination, subtraction, or intersection of multiple meshes. By applying the Boolean modifier, you can create complex shapes that would be difficult to model using traditional techniques. The Boolean operations include Union, Difference, and Intersect, each serving a different purpose. For instance, Union combines two or more objects into a single mesh, while Difference removes one mesh from another, creating a cutout effect. Intersect retains only the overlapping volume of the meshes. The Boolean modifier is particularly useful for creating complex mechanical parts or intricate architectural features.

Managing topology is a crucial aspect of advanced modeling, especially when preparing models for animation. Good topology ensures that the mesh deforms correctly during animation and avoids common issues such as stretching or collapsing. The key principles of good topology include maintaining quads (four-sided polygons) rather than n-gons (polygons with more than four sides), avoiding long, thin triangles, and ensuring that edge loops flow naturally with the model's contours. Edge loops are continuous rings of edges around the model that help define the mesh's shape and facilitate smooth deformations.

Another important aspect of managing topology involves retopology, the process of creating a new mesh over an existing one to improve its topology. Retopology is often used in conjunction with sculpting to create a clean, animation-ready mesh from a highly detailed sculpt. Blender offers several tools for retopology, such as the Shrinkwrap modifier, which projects a new mesh onto the surface of the existing one, and the Retopology Tools add-on, which provides features like snapping vertices to the surface and drawing new topology directly onto the mesh.

UV Unwrapping remains a critical process in advanced modeling, especially when preparing models for texturing. Proper UV mapping ensures that textures are applied correctly and without distortion. For complex models, you may need to manually adjust UV seams and islands to achieve the best results. Blender's UV Editor provides various tools for optimizing UV layouts, including options for aligning and packing UV islands to minimize texture stretching and overlapping.

Lastly, texture painting and shader creation are integral to advanced modeling. Texture painting involves applying color and detail directly onto your model's surface, often using UV maps to guide the placement of textures. Blender's Texture Paint mode allows for painting directly on the 3D model, providing real-time feedback. Shader creation, on the other hand, involves defining the material properties of your model, such as reflectivity, transparency, and bumpiness. Blender's Shader Editor provides a node-based interface for creating complex shaders, allowing you to blend textures, control material properties, and achieve a wide range of visual effects.

With these advanced techniques, you will be well-equipped to tackle complex modeling projects and create detailed, optimized models ready for further development, including animation and rendering. Understanding and applying these methods will enhance your proficiency in Blender and expand your creative possibilities in 3D modeling.

To further enhance your modeling toolkit, we delve into the intricacies of Retopology, a technique crucial for optimizing and refining high-resolution models created through sculpting or other advanced methods. Retopology involves creating a new, lower-resolution mesh over the existing high-resolution model to produce a cleaner, more animation-friendly topology. This process is essential for ensuring that the model deforms correctly during animation and performs efficiently in real-time applications.

The process of retopology often starts with the creation of a new mesh that conforms to the contours of the high-resolution model. Blender provides several tools to facilitate this, including the Shrinkwrap Modifier, which allows the new mesh to conform to the surface of the high-resolution model. The Retopology Tool itself includes features like Snap to Face, which aligns vertices of the new mesh to the underlying high-resolution geometry, ensuring accurate placement and minimizing distortion. Additionally, tools like Polygroups and Vertex Groups can be used to manage different sections of the mesh, making the retopology process more manageable.

When creating a new mesh for retopology, it is important to maintain a clean and organized edge flow. This involves creating loops and rings that follow the natural contours and joints of the model, ensuring that the topology supports smooth deformation. Proper edge flow is particularly important for animating characters, as it affects how well the mesh bends and stretches. Keeping edge loops around areas that require more flexibility, such as joints, and using denser geometry in areas of detail, ensures that the model performs well during animation.

The UV Mapping process also requires special attention in advanced modeling. Proper UV mapping ensures that textures are accurately applied to the model and prevents issues such as stretching or misalignment. When dealing with complex models, unwrapping and laying out UVs can become more intricate. Blender's UV Unwrapping Tools offer several methods to handle this complexity, including Smart UV Project and Unwrap. For complex models, you may need to manually place seams and adjust UV islands to achieve the best results. Using UV Pinning and Live Unwrap features can help maintain a consistent UV layout as you adjust the model.

Another advanced technique is the use of Displacement Maps. Displacement maps are grayscale images that affect the surface of a model by modifying its geometry according to the brightness of the image. This technique is particularly useful for adding fine details to surfaces without significantly increasing the polygon count. In Blender, displacement maps are applied through the Displace Modifier or by using them in the material shaders. Properly setting up displacement maps involves configuring the map's strength and scale to match the model's dimensions and resolution.

Managing Complex Meshes efficiently is also crucial in advanced modeling. As models become more intricate, performance and organization can become challenging. Blender's Mesh Analysis Tools allow you to check for issues such as non-manifold geometry, overlapping faces, and inconsistent normals. Tools like Clean Up and Decimate Modifier help in reducing unnecessary geometry while maintaining the model's appearance. Proper mesh organization, including the use of Collections and Layers, ensures that complex scenes remain manageable and that components are easily accessible.

Finally, understanding and utilizing Vertex Groups and Weight

Painting are essential for preparing models for animation. Vertex Groups allow you to assign specific vertices to different groups, which can then be influenced by armatures or shape keys. Weight Painting is used to control how these vertex groups deform during animation, allowing for precise control over mesh deformation. Proper weight painting ensures smooth transitions and natural movements in animated models, avoiding issues like unnatural distortions or clipping.

By integrating these advanced techniques into your modeling workflow, you can achieve a higher level of detail and functionality in your 3D models. Mastery of sculpting, retopology, UV mapping, displacement maps, and mesh management ensures that your models are not only visually impressive but also optimized for practical use in animations and real-time applications. Each technique contributes to a comprehensive understanding of advanced modeling, providing you with the tools needed to tackle complex projects and refine your skills further.

Displacement Maps offer a sophisticated way to enhance surface detail by modifying the mesh based on grayscale textures. These textures influence the height of the mesh's surface, creating intricate details without the need for a high-resolution base mesh. To utilize displacement maps effectively, first ensure that your model has a sufficient base mesh resolution to handle the detail without excessive distortion. Apply the displacement map through the Displacement Modifier in Blender, adjusting parameters such as Midlevel and Scale to fine-tune the effect. The Displacement Modifier can be combined with Subdivision Surface to achieve even greater detail, allowing for a more refined and nuanced surface.

Managing Topology is integral to creating efficient and animation-ready models. Proper topology involves arranging the mesh's vertices, edges, and faces in a way that supports smooth deformations and minimizes issues during animation.

This includes creating edge loops around areas of articulation, such as joints and facial features, to ensure natural movement. For example, edge loops around the eyes, mouth, and limbs help maintain smooth deformation during character animation. Additionally, the use of Quad-based Meshes is preferred over triangles for animation, as quads generally deform more predictably.

Topology Optimization also includes minimizing Pole and Ngon occurrences. Poles are vertices connected to more or fewer than four edges, which can create artifacts in animation. Ngons, or faces with more than four vertices, can cause problems in rendering and animation due to their unpredictable behavior. Ensuring a clean, quad-based topology not only improves the model's deformation but also enhances its performance in various applications, from real-time rendering to complex simulations.

In the realm of Complex Mesh Management, Blender's Decimate Modifier can be invaluable for reducing the polygon count of a model while preserving its overall shape. This is particularly useful for optimizing models for real-time applications or for use in environments where performance is critical. The Decimate Modifier offers several options, including Collapse, Un-Subdivide, and Planar, each suited to different types of mesh reduction. Adjusting these settings allows you to strike a balance between detail and performance, ensuring your model remains both detailed and efficient.

Another advanced technique involves the Use of Advanced Texturing Techniques, such as Normal Mapping and Bump Mapping, to enhance the visual detail of a model without increasing its polygon count. Normal maps are textures that store normal vector information, altering how light interacts with the surface and creating the illusion of detailed geometry. Bump maps, similar in concept, use grayscale textures to simulate surface texture variations. Both techniques can be used in conjunction with displacement maps to achieve a highly detailed and realistic appearance while maintaining a manageable polygon count.

For Animation Optimization, it's crucial to consider Rigging and Skinning techniques. Rigging involves creating a skeleton structure for your model, which defines how it moves and deforms. Blender's Armature system allows you to build bones and create an armature that can be used to control your model's movements. Skinning, or weight painting, assigns how much influence each bone has on different parts of the mesh. This process ensures smooth deformations and helps avoid issues like mesh tearing or unnatural movement during animation. Proper rigging and skinning are essential for ensuring that your model performs well under various poses and animations.

Additionally, Shape Keys can be used to create facial expressions or other deformations that are not easily achieved through rigging alone. Shape keys allow you to define different shapes or expressions and blend them together to create dynamic and expressive animations. This technique is particularly useful for character modeling, where subtle facial movements and expressions are crucial for conveying emotion and personality.

In summary, advanced modeling in Blender encompasses a variety of techniques and tools designed to create intricate and optimized models. Mastery of sculpting, modifiers, retopology, UV mapping, and advanced texturing techniques is essential for producing high-quality, animation-ready models. Managing topology and optimizing models for performance ensures that your creations are not only visually compelling but also functional and efficient for real-time applications and complex animations. By employing these advanced methods, you can achieve a higher level of detail and refinement in your 3D models, paving the way for successful and professional-quality work.

CHAPTER 4: INTRODUCTION TO TEXTURING

Texturing is a pivotal aspect of 3D modeling that transforms your digital creations from mere shapes into vivid, lifelike representations. This process involves applying colors, patterns, and detailed surface information to your models, significantly enhancing their realism and visual appeal. In this segment, we will delve into the essentials of UV mapping and texturing within Blender, covering the fundamental techniques required to unwrap models, apply textures, and use materials and shaders to achieve high-quality results.

The first step in texturing is UV Mapping, which involves projecting a 3D model's surface onto a 2D plane. This projection allows textures to be correctly applied to the model by defining how a 2D image wraps around its 3D surface. The UV mapping process begins with Unwrapping your model, a technique that unfolds the 3D mesh into a flat 2D layout. In Blender, this is achieved by entering Edit Mode, selecting the entire mesh or specific parts, and then using the Unwrap function. The unwrapped UV map, often referred to as a UV layout, represents the model's surface in a 2D format, with the texture applied to it as a guide for mapping.

The UV Editor in Blender is a crucial tool for visualizing and editing the UV layout. Here, you can adjust the placement of

UV islands, which are segments of the UV map corresponding to different areas of the model's surface. Proper alignment of UV islands is essential to avoid texture stretching and ensure that textures fit seamlessly across the model. The UV Editor also allows you to use various tools to manipulate UV coordinates, such as Move, Scale, and Rotate, facilitating precise adjustments and optimization of the UV layout.

Once the UV map is prepared, you can apply textures to the model. Textures are images that define the surface appearance of your model, including details such as color, bumpiness, and reflectivity. In Blender, textures are applied through the Materials system. Each material consists of various properties that control how textures are displayed on the model. To create and assign a material, open the Materials Properties panel, click on New, and then define the material's properties, such as its base color and texture maps.

To apply a texture, you need to add it to the material's Base Color property. This is done by selecting Image Texture from the material's Surface settings and loading the desired texture image. The texture is then mapped to the model based on the UV coordinates. Adjustments can be made to ensure that the texture aligns correctly with the model, using the Mapping settings to tweak the scale, rotation, and position of the texture on the surface.

Materials and Shaders further enhance the visual quality of your models. While textures provide surface detail, shaders define how the material interacts with light. Blender offers a powerful node-based material system known as Cycles and Eevee render engines, which utilize shaders to create complex materials. The Shader Editor allows for detailed control over material properties through nodes, which can be connected to create intricate material setups.

For example, the Principled BSDF Shader is a versatile shader that combines multiple properties into a single node, making it easier to create realistic materials. It includes settings for base color, roughness, metallicity, and more. By adjusting these parameters, you can simulate various materials, such as metals, plastics, or fabrics. Additional texture maps, such as Normal Maps and Specular Maps, can be connected to the shader to provide extra detail and control over how light interacts with the surface.

In addition to these basics, Blender also supports advanced texturing techniques, such as Bump Mapping and Displacement Mapping, which add surface detail without modifying the underlying geometry. Bump mapping uses a grayscale image to create the illusion of surface texture, while displacement mapping modifies the actual geometry based on a texture, allowing for more detailed and realistic surfaces.

Finally, understanding the interplay between UV mapping, textures, and shaders is crucial for achieving high-quality results. By mastering these elements, you can create models that not only look visually compelling but also perform well in various rendering scenarios. Effective texturing requires careful attention to detail, from unwrapping and mapping textures accurately to adjusting material properties and shaders to achieve the desired effect.

In Blender, texturing involves several steps to ensure that the textures align correctly with your 3D models. After you've set up your UV map and created a material, the next crucial step is Texture Painting. Texture painting allows you to directly paint textures onto your model within Blender, which can be particularly useful for creating custom details and ensuring that the texture maps align perfectly with the model's surface.

To begin texture painting, you need to create a paint layer. This is done by adding a new texture to your material and configuring it to be used as a paint layer. In the Texture Properties panel, add a new texture and set its type to Image or Movie. After creating the texture, you need to unwrap your model if you haven't already, as the UV map will determine how the texture is applied. With your model selected, switch to Texture Paint mode, which provides a variety of painting tools and brushes.

The Texture Paint Workspace in Blender includes essential tools such as the Brush Tool, which lets you paint directly onto the model's surface. You can adjust various brush settings, including size, strength, and texture, to achieve the desired effect. The Clone Brush can be particularly useful for copying texture details from one area of the model to another. Additionally, the Masking Tools help you to isolate areas of the model you wish to paint, preventing unwanted texture application.

Baking Textures is another advanced technique that plays a crucial role in optimizing textures for use in various environments. Baking involves transferring detailed texture information from a high-resolution model to a lower-resolution model, which is essential for game engines and real-time rendering. This process includes baking Diffuse Maps, Normal Maps, and Specular Maps, among others. To bake textures in Blender, you first need to create an appropriate UV layout for the lower-resolution model. Then, in the Bake section of the Render Properties panel, specify the type of texture to bake and the target image where the baked texture will be saved. The baking process generates textures that can be applied to your model, preserving the high-resolution detail in a more performance-friendly format.

Materials and Shaders further enhance the appearance of your model by defining how textures interact with light and how they are rendered. Blender provides a powerful node-based system for creating and managing materials and shaders. Within the Shader Editor, you can use Nodes to build complex shading networks. The Principled BSDF Shader is a versatile node that combines multiple shading functions into a single shader, making it ideal for a wide range of materials, from metals to plastics. By connecting textures and adjusting parameters within the Principled BSDF node, you can simulate realistic surface properties such as roughness, metallicity, and translucency.

To further refine the visual quality of your model, you might use additional shaders such as Emission Shaders for creating self-lighting effects or Transparent Shaders for materials that require transparency. The Shader Editor allows for extensive customization, enabling you to create materials that mimic real-world surfaces with high precision. Each shader and texture node can be adjusted to control how light interacts with the surface, enhancing the model's realism.

Properly managing Texture Coordinates is also vital for accurate texture mapping. The UV Map coordinates dictate how a texture is projected onto the model's surface. Blender provides various mapping options, such as Box Projection, Cylindrical Projection, and Spherical Projection, each suited for different modeling scenarios. Choosing the right mapping technique ensures that textures are applied seamlessly, avoiding issues such as stretching or misalignment.

Finally, Texture Optimization is crucial for ensuring that your textures perform well across different platforms and rendering engines. Large textures can significantly impact performance, so it is essential to balance texture resolution with the level of detail required. Using Texture Atlases, which combine multiple textures into a single image, can help manage texture sizes and reduce the number of texture files used in your project. This technique is particularly useful in game development, where performance optimization is critical.

By mastering these advanced texturing techniques, you will be well-equipped to create highly detailed and visually stunning models. Understanding how to effectively unwrap your models, apply and paint textures, and use materials and shaders will significantly enhance the realism and quality of your 3D creations, preparing them for a wide range of applications from animations to interactive environments.

Materials and shaders are integral to achieving the final look and feel of your textured models. In Blender, materials are used to define the surface properties of your 3D objects, such as color, reflectivity, and texture. The Shader Editor is the primary workspace for creating and managing materials, allowing you to utilize a node-based system to configure material properties. This editor enables the combination of various shaders and textures to create complex material effects.

Within the Shader Editor, you'll work with nodes to define how materials interact with light. The Principled BSDF Shader is one of the most versatile shaders available, providing a wide range of settings to control the appearance of the material. It combines multiple shading models, including diffuse, specular, and transmission, into a single node. This shader allows you to adjust parameters such as Base Color, Roughness, Specular, and Metallic, enabling you to create materials that range from matte and rough to glossy and reflective.

The Texture Coordinate node and the Mapping node are essential for managing how textures are applied to your model. The Texture Coordinate node provides different types of coordinate systems, such as UV, Object, and Global, which determine how the texture is projected onto the model. The Mapping node allows you to adjust the position, rotation, and scale of the texture coordinates, providing finer control over the placement and tiling of textures. These nodes are crucial for ensuring that textures align correctly and appear as intended on the 3D model.

Another powerful feature in Blender's material system is the ability to use Image Textures. These textures are applied through the Image Texture node, which can be connected to various shader inputs. By using Image Textures, you can add complex details such as patterns, logos, and surface imperfections to your model. The UV Map generated earlier is used by the Image Texture node to ensure that the texture aligns correctly with the model's surface.

For realistic rendering, Bump Maps and Normal Maps are employed to add surface detail without increasing the mesh's polygon count. Bump Maps use grayscale images to simulate surface irregularities by altering the way light interacts with the surface. Normal Maps, on the other hand, provide more detailed surface information by encoding normal vectors in an RGB image, resulting in more complex surface effects. To apply a bump or normal map, connect the Bump or Normal Map node to the shader's Normal input. Adjust the strength and influence of the map to achieve the desired level of detail.

Additionally, Specular Maps and Roughness Maps control how light reflects off the model's surface. Specular maps dictate the intensity of specular highlights, while roughness maps determine how glossy or matte the surface appears. By using these maps, you can create materials with varying degrees of reflectivity and surface texture, enhancing the realism of your model.

As you progress in texturing, it's important to keep in mind Performance Optimization. High-resolution textures and complex materials can impact rendering times and real-time performance. To mitigate this, consider using Texture Compression, which reduces texture file sizes without significant loss of quality. Additionally, Level of Detail (LOD) techniques can be employed to adjust the texture resolution based on the model's distance from the camera, ensuring that only necessary detail is rendered.

Finally, to achieve realistic results, Lighting and Rendering Settings play a crucial role. Proper lighting setups enhance the appearance of your textures and materials by interacting with them in a way that mimics real-world lighting conditions. Experiment with different types of lights, such as Point Lights, Sun Lights, and Area Lights, to see how they affect your model's appearance. The Render Engine you choose, whether it's Cycles for ray tracing or Eevee for real-time rendering, will also influence how textures and materials are displayed in the final render.

By mastering these texturing techniques and tools, you will be well-equipped to create visually compelling and realistic 3D models. The combination of effective UV mapping, texture painting, and advanced material and shader setups will significantly enhance the quality of your models and prepare them for a variety of applications, from still images to interactive 3D environments.

CHAPTER 5:
LIGHTING BASICS

Lighting plays a fundamental role in defining the mood and atmosphere of your 3D scenes, influencing how objects are perceived and how emotions are conveyed. Properly implemented lighting not only highlights the details of your models but also enhances the overall visual narrative. In this discussion, we will explore the various types of lights available in Blender, their effects on scenes, and the principles of effective lighting design. We will also address techniques for placing and adjusting lights to achieve both realistic and artistically compelling results.

Blender offers several types of lights, each with distinct characteristics and uses. The Point Light is a versatile type that emits light uniformly in all directions from a single point. This light type simulates an idealized bulb or light source and is useful for creating general illumination in a scene. However, it is important to consider that Point Lights can produce soft shadows if not managed correctly. Adjusting the Intensity and Radius parameters allows you to control the light's brightness and the spread of its illumination.

The Sun Light is designed to replicate the light emitted by the sun, providing parallel rays of light. This light source is ideal for creating outdoor environments or scenes where a consistent, directional light is needed. The Sun Light does not have a defined location but rather casts light from a specified direction, making it suitable for simulating daylight. By adjusting the Angle parameter, you can control the softness of the shadows cast by this light source, which is crucial for achieving realistic outdoor lighting.

Spot Lights emit light in a cone-shaped beam, focusing illumination on a specific area. This light type is particularly useful for creating dramatic effects, highlighting particular objects, or simulating stage lighting. The Spot Light allows you to adjust the Spot Size and Blend parameters to control the spread and softness of the light. By manipulating these settings, you can create focused light with a sharp cutoff or a more gradual transition from light to shadow.

Area Lights simulate light sources with a defined surface area, such as fluorescent panels or softboxes. Unlike Point Lights and Spot Lights, Area Lights produce soft shadows with smooth gradients, making them ideal for simulating diffused lighting conditions. The size and shape of the light source can be adjusted through the Size and Shape parameters, which affect how light is distributed and how shadows are cast. For instance, increasing the Size of an Area Light will result in softer shadows with less pronounced edges, mimicking the effect of a large light source.

In Blender, the effective placement and adjustment of lights are critical for achieving the desired visual impact. Light Placement involves positioning your lights in a manner that highlights the important features of your scene while creating a balanced and visually appealing composition. The Three-Point Lighting technique is a fundamental method that utilizes three types of lights to create a well-rounded illumination setup: the Key Light, the Fill Light, and the Back Light.

The Key Light is the primary light source, responsible for casting the main shadows and defining the subject's form. It is typically placed at an angle to the subject to create dynamic lighting effects and emphasize texture. The Fill Light is positioned on the opposite side of the Key Light, with a softer intensity, to reduce the harsh shadows cast by the Key Light and provide additional illumination to the shadowed areas. Finally, the Back Light, or Rim Light, is placed behind the subject to create a rim or halo effect, helping to separate the subject from the background and add depth to the scene.

Lighting Design Principles involve understanding how light interacts with objects and surfaces to enhance the storytelling of your scene. Key principles include Contrast, which refers to the difference between light and dark areas, and Color Temperature, which affects the mood of the scene by influencing the warmth or coolness of the light. By manipulating these principles, you can evoke specific emotions or highlight particular aspects of your scene. For example, high contrast lighting with harsh shadows can create a dramatic and intense atmosphere, while soft, diffused lighting with warm color temperatures can evoke a cozy and inviting feeling.

Experimentation is essential for mastering lighting techniques. Adjusting the intensity, color, and position of lights in your scene allows you to explore various effects and refine your approach to achieve the desired visual outcome. Blender's real-time rendering preview enables you to see the immediate impact of lighting adjustments, facilitating iterative experimentation and fine-tuning.

Understanding and implementing effective lighting techniques is crucial for creating visually engaging and emotionally impactful 3D scenes. By mastering the different types of lights, their placement, and the principles of lighting design, you can enhance the realism and narrative quality of your animations, making your models come to life with compelling illumination.

The placement and adjustment of lights in a scene are crucial for achieving desired effects and conveying the right atmosphere. When positioning lights, you must consider how their placement affects the scene's composition, shadows, and overall illumination. For instance, placing a Point Light in the center of a room can create a general light source that evenly illuminates the space. However, to highlight specific features or create dramatic contrasts, you might position the light closer to or farther from certain objects, adjusting the Intensity and Radius to control the spread and strength of the light.

When using Sun Lights, it's essential to consider the angle at which the light is cast. The direction of the sun affects the length and orientation of shadows, which can significantly influence the scene's mood. For example, a low-angle sun can create long, dramatic shadows that evoke a sense of time, such as early morning or late afternoon. Adjusting the Angle parameter allows you to simulate different times of day or atmospheric conditions, affecting the softness and length of the shadows.

Spot Lights are particularly useful for creating emphasis or guiding the viewer's attention. By adjusting the Spot Size and Blend parameters, you can control the focus and falloff of the light beam. This allows you to spotlight specific objects or characters in a scene while keeping the rest of the environment in relative darkness. Effective use of Spot Lights can direct the viewer's gaze and enhance narrative focus, making them a powerful tool for storytelling in animations.

Area Lights provide a more diffused lighting effect, making them ideal for simulating soft, natural light sources like the sun's ambient light or a studio softbox. The Size and Shape of the Area Light determine how the light is distributed and how shadows are cast. Larger lights produce softer shadows and more even illumination, while smaller lights create sharper shadows and more focused light. Adjusting these parameters helps achieve a more natural look, especially in scenes requiring even and gentle lighting.

Beyond the basic types of lights, Lighting Design Principles play a significant role in crafting visually compelling scenes. Key principles include Three-Point Lighting, which involves using a Key Light, a Fill Light, and a Back Light to create balanced illumination and enhance depth. The Key Light is the primary light source and provides the main illumination, while the Fill Light softens the shadows created by the Key Light and reduces contrast. The Back Light, or Rim Light, adds separation between the subject and the background, highlighting edges and creating a sense of depth.

Another principle is Lighting Ratio, which refers to the balance between different light sources and their intensities. Adjusting the lighting ratio helps control the contrast in the scene and influences the overall mood. For example, a high contrast ratio with strong key and fill lights can create a dramatic, intense look, while a lower contrast ratio with more balanced lighting can result in a softer, more natural appearance.

Color Temperature is also a critical aspect of lighting design. The color temperature of a light source affects the warmth or coolness of the scene, influencing its emotional tone. Warm Light (typically with a color temperature below 3200K) can create a cozy, inviting atmosphere, while Cool Light (above 5000K) gives a more clinical, crisp feeling. Adjusting the color temperature allows you to match the lighting to the scene's context, whether it's a warm indoor setting or a cool, outdoor environment.

Light Intensity and Falloff settings are vital for controlling how light diminishes over distance. The intensity determines how bright the light source is, while falloff controls how quickly the light fades as it moves away from the source. Understanding these settings helps in creating realistic lighting conditions, simulating how light naturally diminishes and ensuring that distant objects are adequately illuminated or appropriately shaded.

Finally, integrating Lighting Effects such as Volumetric Lighting and Gobo Shadows can add an extra layer of realism and artistic flair to your scene. Volumetric Lighting creates the appearance of light beams filtering through the air, adding depth and atmosphere. Gobo Shadows involve projecting patterns or textures onto the scene using a light, which can be used to simulate effects like dappled sunlight or create interesting shadow patterns.

By mastering these lighting techniques and principles, you can enhance the visual quality and narrative impact of your 3D scenes. Effective lighting not only illuminates your models but also plays a crucial role in storytelling, helping to guide the viewer's attention and evoke the desired emotional response.

The Three-Point Lighting technique is a foundational method in lighting design, crucial for creating a well-lit and dynamic scene. This technique involves the strategic placement of three different types of lights: the Key Light, the Fill Light, and the Back Light. Each of these lights serves a distinct purpose and together they form a balanced illumination that highlights your subject while providing depth and dimension.

The Key Light is the primary light source and is typically the most intense and directional. It establishes the main light and shadow pattern on the subject, setting the overall mood of the scene. Placement of the Key Light is crucial—it should be positioned at a 45-degree angle to the subject, both horizontally and vertically, to achieve a natural and visually appealing look. Adjusting its intensity and angle will affect how shadows fall and how features are highlighted.

The Fill Light complements the Key Light by reducing the contrast created by the shadows. It is softer and less intense, designed to fill in the shadows without eliminating them entirely. The Fill Light should be positioned on the opposite side of the Key Light, at a lower intensity, to ensure that the shadows are softened rather than completely removed. This helps to reveal the details in the shadowed areas while maintaining a natural look.

The Back Light, also known as the Rim Light, is placed behind the subject and aimed towards the camera. Its primary role is to separate the subject from the background by creating a rim of light around the edges. This separation enhances the subject's depth and helps it stand out against the background. The Back Light should be set at an appropriate intensity to create a visible rim effect without overpowering the Key and Fill Lights.

Effective lighting design also involves understanding the Color Temperature of lights. In Blender, the color temperature can be adjusted using the Color settings within the light properties. Different color temperatures can evoke different moods; for instance, warmer colors (around 3000K) create a cozy, inviting atmosphere, while cooler colors (around 6000K) can produce a more sterile or daylight feel. Balancing color temperatures between lights can help in achieving a harmonious and visually coherent scene.

Another essential aspect of lighting design is the manipulation of Shadow Types and their qualities. Blender provides several shadow options, including Hard Shadows and Soft Shadows. Hard Shadows have a sharp, well-defined edge, creating a more dramatic and high-contrast effect. They are typically used in scenes where strong, directional light sources are desired. Soft Shadows, on the other hand, have a gradual transition from light to dark, resulting in a more natural and diffused effect. This type of shadow is achieved using larger light sources or by increasing the light's size and distance from the subject.

To further enhance realism and control, Blender offers additional lighting features such as Light Falloff and Light Groups. Light Falloff controls how the intensity of light diminishes over distance. By adjusting the Falloff Type and Distance parameters, you can create lights that mimic real-world behavior, such as the diminishing light of a distant source or the focused beam of a spotlight. Light Groups allow for the organization of multiple lights into groups, making it easier to manage and adjust lighting setups, especially in complex scenes.

As you develop your lighting skills, it is important to experiment with different lighting setups and techniques to understand their impact on your scene. Practicing with various light types, placements, and intensities will give you a better grasp of how lighting affects mood, atmosphere, and visual storytelling. Use the principles of lighting design not just to illuminate your scene, but to enhance the narrative and emotional impact of your work.

In summary, mastering lighting in Blender involves understanding the characteristics and applications of different light types, learning how to strategically place and adjust lights, and applying principles of effective lighting design. By combining these techniques, you can create visually compelling and realistic 3D scenes that effectively convey your intended mood and storytelling objectives.

CHAPTER 6:
CAMERA SETUP AND COMPOSITION

The camera plays a pivotal role in animation, serving as the viewer's eyes and significantly influencing how a scene is perceived. Proper camera setup and composition are essential for effective storytelling, as they guide the viewer's focus, establish mood, and enhance the narrative. In this exploration, I will cover the fundamentals of positioning and animating cameras in Blender, and provide techniques for framing shots and creating dynamic movements that enrich your animations.

To begin with, setting up a camera in Blender involves understanding both its position and orientation within the 3D space. By default, a new camera is positioned at the origin of the scene, facing along the negative Z-axis. Adjusting the Camera Location and Rotation parameters allows you to reposition and reorient the camera to achieve the desired perspective. You can move the camera along the X, Y, and Z axes using the Transform panel or by directly manipulating the camera in the 3D Viewport. The camera's orientation can be adjusted by rotating it, which changes the angle at which it views the scene.

One of the most critical aspects of camera setup is Focal Length, which influences the camera's field of view and perspective. A shorter focal length (wide-angle) captures a broader view of the scene, exaggerating the sense of depth and making objects appear further apart. Conversely, a longer focal length (telephoto) narrows the field of view, compressing the scene and bringing objects closer together. Adjusting the focal length allows you to control the composition of your shots and the overall visual impact.

The Depth of Field (DoF) effect is another important aspect of camera setup, adding a layer of realism and focus to your scenes. By enabling Depth of Field, you can control the Focus Distance, which determines which parts of the scene are in sharp focus and which are blurred. This effect mimics how real-world cameras handle focus, drawing attention to specific elements and enhancing the cinematic quality of your animation. Adjusting the F-Stop value changes the size of the aperture, affecting the amount of blur in the out-of-focus areas.

Framing your shots effectively is crucial for guiding the viewer's attention and conveying the intended message. Rule of Thirds is a fundamental compositional technique where the frame is divided into a 3x3 grid. Key elements of the scene should be positioned along the lines or at their intersections, creating a balanced and engaging composition. This technique helps in placing the main subject off-center, providing a more dynamic and interesting view.

Leading Lines is another compositional technique that uses natural or created lines within the scene to direct the viewer's eye towards the main subject. Lines can be physical elements like roads, beams, or paths, or they can be implied through the arrangement of objects and lighting. Leading lines create a sense of depth and perspective, making the scene more immersive and visually appealing.

When it comes to Camera Movement, animating the camera can add a dynamic element to your scenes, enhancing storytelling and emotional impact. Dolly Moves involve moving the camera closer to or farther from the subject, changing the perspective and focus. Pan Moves involve rotating the camera horizontally, which is effective for following action or revealing additional parts of the scene. Tilt Moves rotate the camera vertically, which can highlight changes in elevation or the height of objects.

Tracking Shots involve moving the camera along a predefined path, often using the Path Animation feature in Blender. This technique allows the camera to follow a subject or traverse the scene in a smooth and controlled manner. Creating a path for the camera and adjusting its movement can help in achieving complex camera movements that add drama or interest to your animation.

In addition to these techniques, understanding the concept of Camera Framing is vital for ensuring that your scenes are well-composed. This involves adjusting the camera's position and angle to frame the subject effectively, considering elements such as Headroom, Leadroom, and Negative Space. Headroom ensures that there is enough space above the subject's head, avoiding a cramped look. Leadroom provides space in the direction the subject is facing or moving, giving a sense of movement or anticipation. Negative Space refers to the empty space around the subject, which can help in emphasizing the subject and creating a balanced composition.

By mastering these techniques and principles, you can effectively control how your scenes are viewed and perceived, enhancing the overall quality of your animations. Whether it's through precise camera placement, effective framing, or dynamic movements, the way you handle the camera will significantly impact the storytelling and visual appeal of your work.

An effective method for achieving balanced and engaging compositions is to employ the Rule of Thirds. This technique divides the image into a 3x3 grid, creating nine equal sections. By positioning the key elements of your scene along these lines or at their intersections, you create a more dynamic and visually interesting composition. This approach helps to avoid centering the subject, which can often result in a static and less engaging shot. In Blender, you can overlay this grid on your viewport or use the built-in guides to assist with placement.

Another vital compositional technique is the use of Leading Lines. Leading lines are natural or artificial lines within the scene that direct the viewer's eye towards the main subject. These lines can be roads, bridges, or even shadows. By incorporating leading lines into your camera setup, you guide the viewer's attention and enhance the sense of depth and perspective. Adjusting the camera's position and angle to make the most of these lines can dramatically improve the visual impact of your scene.

Camera Angles also play a crucial role in storytelling. Different angles can convey various emotions and perspectives. For instance, a low-angle shot, where the camera is positioned below the subject looking up, can make the subject appear more imposing or heroic. Conversely, a high-angle shot, where the camera is positioned above the subject looking down, can make the subject seem smaller or more vulnerable. Experimenting with these angles can help you find the most effective way to convey the desired mood or narrative.

In addition to static camera setups, Camera Movement adds a dynamic element to your scenes. Blender provides several tools and techniques for animating camera movements. One of the primary methods is to use Keyframes to record the camera's position and orientation at specific points in time. By setting keyframes, you can create smooth transitions between different camera positions and angles. For example, a Dolly or Tracking Shot, where the camera moves towards or away from the subject, can add a sense of motion and depth to the scene.

Another common camera movement technique is the Pan. This involves rotating the camera horizontally while keeping it in a fixed position. A pan can be used to follow the action or reveal additional parts of the scene, creating a sense of continuity and flow. Similarly, a Tilt moves the camera vertically, which can be used to show the height of objects or follow vertical movements.

For more complex movements, such as those involving both rotation and translation, you can use Camera Paths. In Blender, you can create a path using a curve, and then attach the camera to this path. The camera will follow the path as it moves, allowing for intricate and precise camera movements. Adjusting the curve's shape and animation timing provides control over the camera's speed and trajectory, adding a professional touch to your animation.

Understanding Camera Framing is also essential for effective composition. The camera's Field of View (FOV) dictates how much of the scene is visible through the lens. A wider FOV captures more of the scene but may distort objects towards the edges, while a narrower FOV focuses on a smaller area with less distortion. Adjusting the FOV helps to frame the subject appropriately and ensures that the most important elements are included in the shot.

To further refine your scene, Blender's Composition Guides can be employed. These guides include options such as the Golden Ratio, which offers a more complex and aesthetically pleasing compositional framework than the Rule of Thirds. By aligning key elements along the golden ratio's lines and intersections, you can achieve a visually compelling arrangement that is naturally pleasing to the eye.

Lastly, the Camera Depth of Field effect can be utilized to add a layer of realism and focus to your shots. By adjusting the focus distance and aperture settings, you can control the sharpness of the foreground and background, creating a more immersive experience. This effect is particularly useful for highlighting specific elements within the scene while subtly blurring out less important areas, guiding the viewer's attention and enhancing the overall composition.

In summary, mastering camera setup and composition in Blender involves understanding and applying a range of techniques to create visually compelling and narratively effective scenes. By carefully positioning and animating cameras, employing compositional rules and principles, and utilizing dynamic camera movements, you can significantly enhance the storytelling power and visual impact of your animations.

When working with camera angles and movements, the Dolly Zoom effect, also known as the Vertigo effect, is a technique that can create a dramatic change in perspective. This effect involves moving the camera closer or further away from the subject while simultaneously adjusting the focal length to keep the subject the same size in the frame. The result is a visually striking transformation of the background perspective, which can evoke a sense of unease or revelation. In Blender, you achieve this effect by animating both the camera's location and the focal length parameters, ensuring that the background changes proportionally as the camera moves.

In scenes requiring more intricate camera movements, such as following a character or object, utilizing Path Animation is an effective strategy. By creating a curve path that the camera follows, you can achieve smooth, complex camera movements without manually adjusting the camera's position frame by frame. This technique allows for precise control over the camera's trajectory, ensuring consistent movement and eliminating the need for continuous manual adjustments. The curve can be edited to adjust the speed and trajectory of the camera's movement, providing flexibility in how the scene is presented.

Camera Constraints are another valuable tool in Blender for controlling camera behavior. Constraints such as Track To or

Follow Path can automate camera movements and keep the focus on a particular object or follow a pre-defined path. For instance, using the Track To constraint, the camera can be set to always point towards a specific object, maintaining its orientation relative to that object regardless of the camera's position. This is especially useful for scenes where the camera needs to continuously track a moving subject, ensuring that the subject remains in focus and properly framed.

When positioning your camera, it's crucial to consider the Depth of Field effect, which we previously touched upon. Proper management of Depth of Field can significantly enhance the visual appeal of your animation. In Blender, this effect is controlled through the camera settings under the Depth of Field panel. Adjusting the Focus Distance and F-Stop values allows you to dictate which parts of the scene appear in sharp focus and which are blurred, thereby guiding the viewer's attention and creating a more immersive experience. Fine-tuning these settings is essential for achieving a professional-looking result that highlights the focal points of your scene.

Moreover, understanding Lighting and Shadows in relation to camera setup is integral to creating a compelling scene. The interaction between lighting and shadows can affect the perception of depth and the overall mood of the scene. By positioning the camera thoughtfully in relation to light sources, you can accentuate textures and create dynamic shadow play that enhances the scene's realism. It's often beneficial to experiment with different lighting setups and camera angles to find the most visually striking combination.

Camera Animation is not limited to movement alone; transitions between different camera setups can also be animated to create seamless changes in perspective. This can be particularly effective in narrative scenes where the camera needs to shift from one focal point to another, such as from a close-up of a character to a wide shot of the environment. By setting keyframes for different camera positions and smoothly interpolating between them, you can maintain continuity and ensure a smooth visual flow in your animation.

Finally, it is essential to continuously review your camera setups within the context of the animation. Regularly previewing your scene with the camera's perspective allows you to identify any issues with framing or composition early on. Utilizing Blender's Render Preview mode can help you see how lighting, textures, and camera angles work together, allowing for adjustments before the final render. This iterative process of review and refinement is crucial for achieving a polished and visually engaging animation.

By mastering these techniques, you will be well-equipped to create compelling and visually dynamic scenes. The ability to manipulate camera positions, angles, and movements with precision will enhance your storytelling capabilities, allowing you to convey narrative elements effectively and engage your audience more deeply.

CHAPTER 7: INTRODUCTION TO ANIMATION

Animation transforms static models into dynamic visual narratives, making it one of the most compelling aspects of 3D design. In Blender, animating objects involves several fundamental principles and tools that allow for the creation of movement and expression. This section will guide you through the essentials of animation in Blender, focusing on setting up keyframes, managing motion paths, and understanding the basics of fluid and natural movement.

To start animating in Blender, you first need to grasp the concept of keyframes, which are the cornerstone of animation. Keyframes are specific points in time where you define the properties of your objects, such as their location, rotation, or scale. By setting keyframes at different points along the timeline, you create a series of snapshots that Blender uses to interpolate movement between these points. This interpolation creates the illusion of continuous motion. In Blender's Timeline window, you can insert keyframes by selecting the object you wish to animate, adjusting its properties, and pressing `I` to insert a keyframe for the selected property. The timeline allows you to visualize and manage these keyframes, providing a framework within which you can see how your animation progresses over time.

Understanding the Graph Editor is crucial for refining your animations. The Graph Editor in Blender provides a more detailed view of your keyframes by displaying the interpolation curves for various properties. These curves represent the changes in value between keyframes and can be adjusted to refine the timing and smoothness of your animation. By manipulating these curves, you can create more complex and nuanced movements, such as easing in and out, which refers to gradually accelerating or decelerating motion. This principle is key to making animations feel more natural and less mechanical.

To create smooth and realistic movements, it's important to understand motion paths. A motion path visually represents the trajectory of an object as it moves through space over time. In Blender, you can enable motion paths in the 3D Viewport, which allows you to see the path an object follows as it animates. This feature is especially useful for ensuring that the motion is fluid and that the object moves in a way that aligns with your expectations. Adjusting the timing of keyframes and modifying the motion path can help you achieve the desired effect.

Easing is another fundamental concept in animation. It involves varying the speed of an object's movement to create a more realistic effect. Easing can be categorized into two types: easing in and easing out. Easing in refers to starting a motion slowly and then accelerating, while easing out refers to starting quickly and then decelerating towards the end of the motion. Blender's Graph Editor allows you to adjust these easing effects by modifying the curves, making it possible to create animations that feel more natural and less abrupt.

Animating objects in Blender also involves managing the Timeline, which is the primary interface for controlling the duration and sequencing of your animations. The Timeline displays frames and keyframes, allowing you to scrub through your animation and preview the motion. By adjusting the start and end frames, you can control the length of your animation and ensure that it plays within the desired timeframe. Additionally, the Timeline includes playback controls that let you preview your animation in real-time, which is crucial for assessing how well your animation flows and identifying areas that need adjustment.

Another important aspect of animation is the use of Action Editors. These editors allow you to create and manage animation actions, which are sequences of keyframes that can be applied to different objects or characters. In Blender, you can create multiple actions for a single object, making it possible to animate different aspects or states of the object separately. This modular approach to animation helps in organizing complex animations and makes it easier to reuse actions across different projects.

Furthermore, to create more sophisticated animations, you may need to delve into Rigging and Armatures. Rigging involves creating a skeleton or structure for a character or object that allows for complex movements. An armature is a type of rig that provides bones and joints, which can be animated to create realistic motion. Although this topic is more advanced, understanding the basics of rigging is essential for animating characters and other complex objects in Blender.

In summary, animation in Blender involves setting up keyframes, managing motion paths, and applying easing to create natural and fluid movements. Mastering the Timeline, Graph Editor, and understanding concepts like easing and motion paths will enable you to create compelling animations that bring your models to life. As you progress, exploring additional tools such as the Action Editor and rigging techniques will further enhance your ability to create dynamic and intricate animations.

To delve deeper into animation in Blender, it's crucial to

explore the concept of easing, which plays a significant role in enhancing the realism and fluidity of your animations. Easing refers to the gradual acceleration or deceleration of movement, which contrasts with linear motion that remains constant throughout the animation. Easing techniques create more natural and engaging animations by mimicking the way objects move in the real world. In Blender, easing is managed through the Graph Editor, where you can adjust the interpolation of keyframes to achieve smooth transitions.

Blender offers several easing options, including Ease In, Ease Out, and Ease In and Out. Ease In accelerates the object from a standstill, Ease Out decelerates it to a stop, and Ease In and Out combines both, resulting in a smoother start and end to the movement. To apply easing, you can select the keyframes in the Graph Editor and choose the desired easing type from the context menu or use the shortcut keys. By experimenting with these settings, you can fine-tune your animation's timing and create more lifelike motion.

Another essential aspect of animation is understanding animation curves, which represent the changes in an object's properties over time. The Graph Editor's curves provide a visual representation of how properties like location, rotation, and scale change between keyframes. These curves are crucial for fine-tuning animations, as they allow you to see the rate of change and adjust the smoothness of transitions. By manipulating the curve handles, you can refine the motion to be more fluid or abrupt, depending on the desired effect.

In addition to keyframes and easing, motion blur is a technique that enhances the perception of speed and movement in your animations. Motion blur simulates the blurring effect that occurs when objects move quickly, adding realism to the scene. Blender provides various settings to control motion blur, such as the amount of blur and the shutter speed, which can be adjusted in the Render Properties tab. Motion blur is particularly effective in fast-paced scenes where objects or characters are in rapid motion, helping to convey a sense of dynamic movement and energy.

To bring a higher level of realism to your animations, consider incorporating secondary actions, which are subtle movements that complement the primary action. Secondary actions, such as the sway of a character's hair or the ripple of clothing, add depth and nuance to animations. These actions should be synchronized with the main movement and reflect the character's state or the object's interaction with its environment. Adding these details requires careful observation and adjustment but significantly enhances the overall quality of your animation.

Furthermore, anticipation and follow-through are crucial principles in animation that contribute to a more believable and engaging performance. Anticipation involves preparing the audience for an action by performing a smaller, preparatory movement before the main action. For instance, before a character jumps, they might crouch slightly. Follow-through refers to the continuation of movement after the primary action has completed, such as a character's hair or clothing still moving after they have stopped. These techniques help to create a sense of weight and realism in your animations.

Blender's Dope Sheet is another valuable tool for managing and editing animations. The Dope Sheet provides a simplified view of your keyframes, allowing you to see and adjust the timing and placement of these frames across different objects and actions. This tool is particularly useful for making global adjustments to your animation, such as synchronizing multiple elements or changing the duration of an animation sequence.

In summary, mastering animation in Blender involves understanding and applying various techniques and tools to create realistic and engaging movements. Keyframes, easing, motion paths, and animation curves are foundational elements that drive the motion of objects and characters. By refining these elements and incorporating additional techniques such as motion blur, secondary actions, and principles like anticipation and follow-through, you can elevate your animations to a higher level of quality and expressiveness. Each of these components plays a crucial role in achieving fluid, natural, and visually compelling animations that effectively convey the intended message and enhance the storytelling in your projects.

When crafting animations in Blender, it is crucial to master the use of motion paths, which are visual guides that represent the trajectory of an object's movement over time. Motion paths allow you to visualize the path an object follows from one keyframe to another, providing insight into the object's movement and helping to ensure that it follows the intended trajectory. To view motion paths, select the object and navigate to the "Motion Paths" panel within the Object menu. You can generate motion paths for both active and selected keyframes, which are then displayed as a curve in the 3D viewport.

Adjusting these motion paths can significantly enhance the fluidity of your animations. By manipulating the path, you can correct any unintended deviations or refine the arc of motion. For instance, if an object's movement appears too jerky or unnatural, you can smooth out the path by adjusting the keyframes or by using the Graph Editor to modify the associated animation curves. Additionally, motion paths can help in aligning objects within a scene, ensuring that their movements are precise and consistent with the animation's intent.

Furthermore, understanding keyframe interpolation is essential for achieving natural movements. Keyframes, the markers that define specific points in your animation, are interpolated to create transitions between these points. Blender supports various interpolation methods, including linear, Bezier, and constant interpolation. Linear interpolation creates a straight-line transition between keyframes, resulting in uniform motion, while Bezier interpolation provides more control, allowing for smooth acceleration and deceleration through the use of handle adjustments in the Graph Editor. Constant interpolation, on the other hand, maintains the value of the property constant between keyframes, resulting in abrupt changes.

For a more nuanced control over your animations, consider utilizing constraints and parenting. Constraints are powerful tools that limit or guide an object's movement based on predefined rules. For example, a "Track To" constraint can make an object follow or face another object, which is particularly useful for animating cameras or characters. Parenting, on the other hand, involves creating a hierarchical relationship between objects, where one object (the child) inherits the transformations of another (the parent). This technique is invaluable for animating complex rigs, such as character skeletons, where the movement of the parent bones affects the child bones.

As you continue to refine your animations, anticipation and follow-through become crucial elements for creating believable motion. Anticipation involves preparing the audience for an action, such as a character's wind-up before a throw. This pre-action builds up expectation and makes the subsequent movement more convincing. Follow-through refers to the continuation of movement after the main action has ended, such as a character's hair or clothing continuing to move after they have stopped. Both of these principles add realism and depth to your animations, enhancing their overall quality and effectiveness.

Lastly, ensure that you regularly preview and review your animations throughout the process. Blender's timeline and playback features allow you to view your animation in real-time, making it easier to spot any inconsistencies or areas that require adjustment. Utilize the playhead to scrub through your animation and make iterative changes as needed. By frequently previewing your work, you can identify issues early on and make necessary corrections, ensuring that your final animation is polished and fluid.

In summary, animating in Blender involves a comprehensive understanding of keyframes, easing, motion paths, interpolation, constraints, and animation principles. By mastering these elements, you can create animations that are not only technically proficient but also visually engaging and narratively compelling. Practice and experimentation with these techniques will enhance your ability to produce high-quality animations that effectively communicate your creative vision.

CHAPTER 8:
CHARACTER RIGGING

Character rigging is a fundamental step in animating characters, providing them with a skeletal structure that enables movement and deformation. This process is essential for creating believable and fluid animations, as it establishes how a character's mesh interacts with its underlying bones. To start with rigging a character, it's crucial to understand the core components of the rigging process, which include bone creation, weight painting, and control rig setup.

The first step in rigging a character is to create the skeleton or armature, which is the underlying structure that will control the character's movements. In Blender, this begins by adding an Armature object from the Add menu. The Armature is composed of bones that you can position and align to match the character's anatomy. To add bones, enter Edit Mode with the Armature selected and use the Add Bone tool to place and connect bones. It is essential to ensure that the bone structure closely follows the character's joints and limbs, as this will directly affect how the mesh deforms during animation.

Once the skeleton is in place, the next step is weight painting, which determines how the mesh is influenced by the bones. Weight painting assigns weights to the vertices of the mesh, indicating how much influence each bone has over specific parts of the mesh. In Blender, switch to Weight Paint mode with the mesh selected, and then paint weights onto the mesh. The colors displayed represent different levels of influence: red indicates full influence, while blue represents minimal influence. Proper weight painting is crucial for achieving natural and realistic deformations. If the weights are not properly assigned, the mesh may exhibit undesirable distortions or unnatural movements when animated.

After weight painting, you need to set up the control rig, which allows animators to manipulate the character easily. The control rig typically consists of control bones or objects that act as handles for animating the character. These controls are usually placed in strategic locations, such as the character's hands, feet, and facial features, to simplify the animation process. Control rigs can be set up using custom bone shapes or control objects that are parented to the bones of the armature. By using constraints and custom properties, you can enhance the functionality of these controls, making them more intuitive and flexible for animators.

In addition to setting up control rigs, it's important to establish inverse kinematics (IK) and forward kinematics (FK) systems within the rig. Inverse kinematics allows you to manipulate the end of a limb, such as the hand or foot, and automatically adjust the positions of the intermediate joints, making it easier to achieve natural poses. Forward kinematics, on the other hand, involves manipulating the base of the limb and letting the joints follow in sequence. Both systems are useful for different animation scenarios, and incorporating them into your rig will provide greater flexibility and control over your character's movements.

A well-rigged character should also include facial rigging if it requires expressive facial animations. Facial rigging involves creating additional bones or control objects for the character's face to enable movements like blinking, smiling, and frowning. This process often includes creating shape keys or blend shapes that define various facial expressions and can be animated by adjusting sliders. For more complex facial animations, you may need to use a combination of bones, shape keys, and facial rig controls to achieve the desired level of detail and expressiveness.

After completing the rigging process, it's essential to perform thorough testing to ensure that the rig functions correctly and the mesh deforms as expected. Test various poses and animations to identify any issues with bone placement, weight painting, or control rig functionality. Make adjustments as needed to address any problems and ensure that the rigging setup supports the full range of movements required for your character's animations.

By following these steps, you'll create a robust and flexible rig that will serve as the foundation for animating your character. Proper rigging is crucial for achieving high-quality animations and ensuring that your character moves and deforms in a natural and believable manner. As you gain experience with rigging, you'll be able to develop more advanced techniques and refine your skills to handle increasingly complex character rigs and animations.

The process of creating a skeletal structure for character rigging begins with an in-depth understanding of the character's anatomy and the specific movements required for animation. As we continue from setting up the initial armature, it's vital to focus on the bone hierarchy and organization. The hierarchy determines how bones are parented to one another, affecting how movements propagate through the rig. For example, the bones in a character's arm should be parented to the shoulder bone, which is in turn parented to the torso bone. This hierarchical structure ensures that moving one bone, like the shoulder, correctly influences the rest of the arm and hand bones.

In Blender, you manage this hierarchy by selecting bones and using the Parent function to establish relationships between them. Ensure that bones are correctly parented to maintain natural movement; for instance, bending an elbow should also bend the forearm and hand bones. Proper hierarchy setup avoids unwanted deformation and maintains a cohesive animation flow.

After setting up the bone structure, it is crucial to configure the inverse kinematics (IK) and forward kinematics (FK) systems. IK allows for more intuitive control of the character's limbs by automatically calculating the intermediate positions of bones. For example, if you move a character's hand, the IK system will adjust the arm, elbow, and shoulder accordingly. FK, on the other hand, requires the animator to manually adjust each bone from the root to the tip, offering more control over detailed movements. Blender provides tools to switch between IK and FK, giving you flexibility depending on the animation needs.

Once the rig is organized, attention must turn to facial rigging for more expressive animations. Facial rigging involves setting up bones or control objects for facial features such as eyes, mouth, and eyebrows. In Blender, this can be accomplished by adding additional bones specifically for facial expressions and lip-syncing. Custom shape keys or blend shapes can be used in conjunction with these bones to achieve various facial expressions and mouth movements, enhancing the character's emotional range.

Constraint setup is another crucial aspect of character rigging. Constraints help automate certain actions and ensure that the rig behaves predictably. For example, you might use an IK constraint to ensure that a character's feet stay planted on the ground while walking. Constraints can also be applied to control bones to ensure they follow the movement of parent bones correctly. Understanding how to apply and adjust constraints is essential for creating a robust rig that simplifies the animation process.

In addition to constraints, automated rigs can be used to speed up the rigging process. Blender offers several add-ons and tools, such as Rigify, which provide pre-built rigging templates that can be customized for your specific character. These automated rigs offer a starting point, significantly reducing the time and effort required to set up a functional rig. However, it's essential to understand the underlying principles of rigging to effectively customize and troubleshoot these automated rigs.

Finally, after the rigging process is complete, it's vital to perform thorough testing to ensure that the character moves and deforms as expected. This involves animating the character using a variety of poses and actions to check for any issues such as stretching, squashing, or unnatural movements. Testing should be done in various scenarios to ensure the rig performs well under different conditions. Adjustments and refinements are often needed based on the testing results to achieve optimal performance and natural animation.

In summary, effective character rigging in Blender involves meticulous attention to bone structure, weight painting, control rig setup, and constraint management. By following these principles and thoroughly testing the rig, you can create a character that is not only functional but also capable of conveying a wide range of emotions and movements. Rigging is a complex process, but with practice and a solid understanding of these concepts, you can bring your characters to life with compelling and fluid animations.

The final stage in character rigging involves weight painting, a critical process to ensure that your character deforms correctly during animation. Weight painting is the technique used to assign how much influence each bone has on the vertices of your character's mesh. Proper weight painting is essential for achieving natural deformations when the bones are moved.

In Blender, weight painting can be accessed through the Weight Paint mode, which allows you to manually adjust the weight of each vertex by painting directly onto the model. The strength of the influence each bone has on the mesh is represented by different shades of color, with red indicating high influence and blue indicating low influence.

Begin weight painting by selecting a bone and entering Weight Paint mode. You'll notice the model in a color-coded view where you can see the areas of influence. Painting weights involves adjusting brush settings to control the density and falloff of the influence. It is crucial to gradually build up weights to ensure smooth transitions and avoid harsh deformations. Use the "Normalize All" feature to ensure that the weights add up to 1.0 for each vertex, preventing any deformation issues caused by weight imbalances.

As you proceed with weight painting, constantly test the deformation by posing your character in various positions. This iterative process helps identify areas where the weights might need adjustment. Pay particular attention to joints, such as elbows and knees, where complex bending occurs. You may need to tweak weights to avoid undesirable creases or stretching.

In addition to manual weight painting, Blender offers automatic weight generation tools, such as the "Automatic Weights" option in the Armature modifier. This tool calculates initial weights based on the proximity of bones to the mesh, providing a good starting point. However, manual adjustments are often necessary to refine the deformations and achieve the desired results.

Once weight painting is complete, focus on setting up control rigs, which are essential for simplifying animation tasks. Control rigs are a set of specialized controllers or handles that animators use to manipulate the character more easily. These controls abstract the complex bone structure into more intuitive and user-friendly elements.

In Blender, control rigs can be created using custom bones or control shapes. Control shapes are objects like circles or squares that are linked to bones and provide a more convenient interface for animators. For instance, a control shape might be used to handle the character's hand or foot, allowing for precise adjustments without directly manipulating the underlying bones.

Custom properties can also be added to control rigs to enhance their functionality. These properties allow animators to tweak specific parameters, such as muscle bulge or facial expressions, with ease. In Blender, you can add custom properties to bones or control objects through the "Properties" panel, providing a way to add extra functionality to your rig.

It's also important to create rigging presets for frequently used movements or poses. These presets save time by allowing you to quickly apply common rigging configurations or control settings. For instance, you might have a preset for a walking cycle or a specific facial expression that can be applied across different animations.

Throughout the rigging process, testing and refining the rig are crucial. Regularly test your rig by animating it through various poses and movements to ensure that it behaves as expected. Check for issues like unwanted stretching or pinching in the mesh, and make adjustments as needed. Rigging is a balance between technical setup and artistic finesse, so don't hesitate to make iterative changes to achieve the best results.

Finally, documenting your rigging setup is beneficial for future reference and collaboration. Create a detailed rigging guide that outlines the functionality of each control, the weight painting process, and any custom properties or presets you have implemented. This guide will be invaluable for other animators who work with your rig, ensuring a smooth workflow and consistent animation results.

By mastering these rigging techniques, you'll be well-equipped to create versatile and expressive characters that can bring your animations to life.

CHAPTER 9: ANIMATION TECHNIQUES FOR CHARACTERS

Animating a character involves more than just moving it around the screen; it requires creating movements that are believable, engaging, and expressive. This process becomes intricate once your character is rigged and ready for animation. In this section, we'll delve into advanced animation techniques that are essential for bringing characters to life.

To begin with, a fundamental aspect of character animation is the walk cycle. A walk cycle is a series of frames that loop to create the illusion of walking. It is a repeating animation that must convey the natural rhythm and fluidity of human or creature movement. To create a convincing walk cycle, start by studying the mechanics of walking. Observe the way the body shifts weight, the arms swing, and the legs move. The key is to capture the nuances of these movements.

In Blender, begin by setting up your character in a neutral pose, which will act as the starting and ending point of the cycle. Frame this pose as your key pose. The subsequent key poses should reflect the main stages of a walk: the contact pose (when the foot makes contact with the ground), the passing pose (when one leg passes the other), and the up/down poses (when the character is at the peak of the step or in its lowest position).

Once you have these key poses established, you can use interpolation to fill in the intermediate frames. Blender's Graph Editor is invaluable here, allowing you to adjust the animation curves that represent the motion paths of your character. By refining these curves, you can smooth out transitions between key poses and ensure that the walk cycle looks natural.

Facial expressions add another layer of depth to character animation. To animate facial expressions, you can use shape keys (also known as blend shapes) in Blender. Shape keys are a method of deforming the mesh to achieve various expressions. For instance, you might create shape keys for emotions like happiness, sadness, or surprise. By animating these shape keys over time, you can convey a wide range of emotions and reactions.

To begin, create shape keys for each of the desired expressions. Ensure these shape keys are properly set up by adjusting the mesh in edit mode and then assigning these adjustments to individual shape keys. In the animation timeline, you can then keyframe these shape keys to transition between different expressions, adding another layer of believability to your character.

Interactions between characters is another crucial aspect of character animation. This involves animating characters in relation to each other, such as a conversation between two characters or a complex fight scene. To achieve this, focus on timing and spacing, which are essential principles of animation that ensure interactions appear fluid and natural.

In Blender, when animating interactions, you often need to coordinate the actions of multiple characters. This involves careful planning and often requires pose-to-pose animation, where you create key poses for each character at significant points in the interaction. For instance, if characters are shaking hands, you would create key poses for each stage of the handshake, then use the Graph Editor to refine the motion between these key poses.

Animation curves play a pivotal role in refining the smoothness and realism of animations. In Blender's Graph Editor, you can view and adjust the animation curves that represent the motion of your character. Each curve corresponds to a specific property of your character, such as its position or rotation. By manipulating these curves, you can ensure that the animation transitions smoothly between keyframes.

Utilize easing to add realism to your animations. Easing involves adjusting the rate of acceleration and deceleration in your animations. For example, an action like a jump will naturally accelerate as the character starts to rise and decelerate as they begin to fall. By using ease-in and ease-out techniques, you can make movements appear more lifelike and fluid.

Lastly, polishing your animations is an essential step to ensure everything looks as good as possible. This involves reviewing the animation, making adjustments, and ensuring that all elements work together harmoniously. Regular playback and review help identify any issues or areas that need improvement. Refine the details, check the fluidity of the movements, and make sure the animation aligns with the intended emotion or action.

As you work through these techniques, remember that character animation is both an art and a science. It requires a deep understanding of movement mechanics and an artistic touch to convey personality and emotion. By mastering these techniques, you'll be able to create dynamic, engaging animations that bring your characters to life in a compelling and believable way.

When animating characters, interactions between characters present another layer of complexity. Ensuring that characters interact realistically with one another requires careful attention to detail and timing. One of the most critical aspects of this process is synchronization—making sure that the movements and reactions of characters are coherent and timely.

Begin by determining the points of interaction between characters. This might include physical contact, such as one character handing an object to another or characters engaging in a conversation. To effectively animate these interactions, you must first establish the keyframes for each character's action. For example, if two characters are having a dialogue, you'll need to animate their facial expressions, body language, and any hand gestures in sync with each other. Consider how each character's movements influence the other's responses. For instance, if one character moves their hand toward another, the second character should react in a way that feels natural—perhaps shifting their gaze or moving away slightly.

Animation curves are indispensable tools for refining interactions. The Graph Editor in Blender allows you to view and adjust these curves, which represent the animation data for each attribute. By adjusting these curves, you can ensure that movements are smooth and transitions between actions are natural. For example, if a character is reaching for an object, you'll use animation curves to smooth out the motion, making sure that it doesn't appear jerky or unrealistic.

In addition to animation curves, the Dope Sheet provides a broader view of your animation data. It helps you manage and synchronize keyframes across different actions and characters. By utilizing the Dope Sheet, you can easily adjust timing, spacing, and overlap between various movements and interactions, ensuring that your animations maintain consistency and flow.

When animating complex interactions, such as a fight scene or a dance sequence, the use of inverse kinematics (IK) can be particularly useful. IK simplifies the animation process by allowing you to control the movement of a chain of bones from the end effectors. For example, in a fight scene, you can use IK to ensure that a character's hand correctly follows the path of an opponent's body, making the movements more fluid and believable. Conversely, forward kinematics (FK) can be used to animate the movement of individual joints, providing greater control over the character's limbs.

To refine your character animations further, consider incorporating secondary animations. These are subtle movements that occur as a result of primary actions. For example, when a character jumps, their hair, clothes, and other accessories might move in response to the jump. Adding these secondary animations can significantly enhance the realism of your character's movements. Use Blender's Simulations tools, such as cloth simulation for clothing or hair simulation for character hair, to create these additional layers of realism.

Moreover, anticipation and follow-through are essential principles in animation that help to make movements look more natural. Anticipation involves preparing the audience for an action by making a preliminary movement. For instance, before a character jumps, they might crouch slightly to build momentum. Follow-through, on the other hand, refers to the continuation of movement after the main action has been completed. For example, after a character swings a sword, their arm should continue to move naturally, reflecting the force and momentum of the swing.

Finally, feedback and iteration are crucial components of the animation process. Always review your animations critically, both in isolation and within the context of the entire scene. It can be helpful to get feedback from others, as they may notice issues that you might have overlooked. Iteratively refine your animations based on this feedback, adjusting keyframes, curves, and secondary animations as necessary to achieve the most realistic and engaging results.

By mastering these techniques, you can bring a level of depth and realism to your character animations that will captivate your audience and enhance the overall quality of your work. The combination of precise keyframing, thoughtful use of animation curves, effective management of interactions, and attention to detail in secondary animations will enable you to create compelling and lifelike character animations.

When it comes to refining animations, the principles of motion play a crucial role. These principles include concepts such as anticipation, exaggeration, and secondary motion, which are fundamental to making animations look more dynamic and lifelike.

Anticipation involves preparing the audience for an action before it happens. For instance, if a character is about to jump, you might first animate them crouching or preparing their legs. This preparatory movement helps the viewer understand the upcoming action and makes the final jump feel more powerful and realistic. Anticipation is especially important in character animation, as it helps create a sense of weight and effort.

Exaggeration is another key principle, and it involves amplifying movements to make them more expressive and clear. In animation, subtle movements can sometimes get lost, so exaggerating certain actions helps ensure that the audience can easily follow and understand what's happening. For example, if a character is surprised, you might exaggerate their facial expression, widening their eyes and raising their eyebrows more than in real life. This exaggeration makes the emotion more apparent and enhances the overall impact of the animation.

Secondary motion refers to the additional movements that occur as a result of the primary action. These are often smaller, more subtle motions that add realism and fluidity to the animation. For instance, when a character waves their hand, the movement of their arm might cause their clothing or hair to sway slightly. Adding this secondary motion helps to make the animation feel more natural and convincing. In Blender, you can achieve secondary motion by carefully adjusting keyframes and using tools like the Graph Editor to refine the timing and spacing of these additional movements.

The Animation Graph Editor and the Dope Sheet are instrumental in managing and refining your animations. The Graph Editor allows you to view and manipulate animation curves, which represent the changes in your character's attributes over time. By adjusting these curves, you can smooth out transitions and correct any jerky movements. The Dope Sheet provides a broader overview of your animation keyframes, making it easier to synchronize and manage the timing of different actions.

In addition to these tools, Blender's Pose Library is useful for animating repetitive actions or poses. For example, if you need a character to perform a series of similar movements, such as walking or running, you can save these poses in the Pose Library and apply them to different parts of your animation. This approach streamlines the animation process and ensures consistency across various scenes.

Facial animation is another critical aspect of character animation, as it conveys emotions and personality. Creating expressive facial animations requires a deep understanding of the character's emotions and how they translate to facial movements. In Blender, you can use shape keys or blend shapes to create different facial expressions and adjust them as needed. For instance, you might create separate shape keys for smiling, frowning, and raising eyebrows, and then blend these shapes together to achieve the desired expression. Carefully animating these facial expressions can greatly enhance the character's believability and emotional impact.

In the realm of character animation, rig constraints can be used to control and limit the range of motion of various body parts. These constraints help prevent unnatural or undesirable movements and ensure that your character moves within realistic limits. For instance, you might use an IK constraint to ensure that a character's hand follows a specific path, while using FK constraints to control the individual joints of the arm.

Lastly, render previews are essential for assessing the quality of your animation. By rendering out short preview clips, you can review how your animation looks in motion and identify any areas that need adjustment. This iterative process of reviewing and refining your animations helps to ensure that the final product is polished and professional.

In summary, advanced character animation techniques involve a combination of principles, tools, and careful attention to detail. By applying principles such as anticipation, exaggeration, and secondary motion, and using tools like the Graph Editor and Pose Library, you can create animations that are both compelling and realistic. Whether you're animating a walk cycle, facial expressions, or complex interactions between characters, mastering these techniques will significantly enhance the quality of your animations.

Physics Simulations

Physics simulations are a powerful tool in Blender that bring a layer of realism and interactivity to animations. By leveraging Blender's built-in physics engines, you can simulate a range of physical phenomena, including rigid body dynamics, fluid interactions, and cloth behavior. Understanding and mastering these simulations can greatly enhance the believability of your scenes and animations.

Rigid Body Dynamics serve as a fundamental component for simulating objects that interact with each other through physical forces. To begin with, it's essential to understand how rigid body simulations work. Objects are treated as solid bodies that can collide, slide, and bounce off one another based on real-world physics principles. In Blender, you can set up a rigid body simulation by first selecting the objects you wish to simulate. Under the Physics Properties tab, you will find the Rigid Body option, which you can enable to turn your selected objects into dynamic entities.

You have the choice between two types of rigid body simulations: Active and Passive. Active rigid bodies are those that are influenced by forces like gravity and collisions, while Passive rigid bodies are static and only interact with active bodies. For example, if you want to simulate a falling ball hitting the ground, you would set the ball as Active and the ground as Passive. The simulation engine calculates the interaction between these bodies based on their physical properties, such as mass and friction. Adjusting these properties allows you to fine-tune the behavior of the objects. For instance, increasing the friction of the ball will make it roll less smoothly, while a higher mass will result in a more forceful impact.

Next, we delve into fluid simulations, which add another layer of complexity and realism. Fluid simulations in Blender allow you to create scenes where liquids flow, splash, and interact with other objects. To set up a fluid simulation, you first need to define the fluid domain, which is the area where the simulation takes place. This domain is typically represented by a mesh that encapsulates the entire simulation space. Within the Physics Properties tab, you can then add fluid simulation properties to your domain object.

The type of fluid simulation you choose—either liquid or gas —will determine how the fluid behaves. For liquids, you can simulate realistic interactions such as pouring, splashing, and mixing. To control the fluid's behavior, you need to set up fluid objects within the domain, including the fluid emitter (which releases the fluid), and obstacle objects (which the fluid interacts with). Parameters such as fluid viscosity, surface tension, and domain resolution significantly impact the simulation's accuracy and quality. Higher resolution domains produce more detailed simulations but require more computing power.

Cloth simulations add a layer of realism by simulating the movement and deformation of fabric and other flexible materials. These simulations can be used to create realistic clothing, flags, or other soft objects that interact with forces like wind and gravity. To set up a cloth simulation, you need to assign the Cloth physics property to your mesh. Blender allows you to configure various parameters, including the cloth's stiffness, damping, and friction. These settings affect how the cloth reacts to forces and collisions.

To achieve realistic cloth behavior, it is crucial to understand the material properties. For instance, a higher stiffness value will make the cloth less prone to deformation, making it feel more like a rigid material. Conversely, lower stiffness values result in more floppy, flexible behavior. Additionally, the damping setting controls how quickly the cloth's motion slows down, affecting how it settles over time.

Interaction between different simulations often requires careful balancing. For example, if you have both fluid and cloth simulations in a scene, you need to ensure that the fluid's movement properly interacts with the cloth's behavior. This can involve adjusting simulation settings to account for interactions between the fluid's splashes and the cloth's draping.

Finally, simulation caching plays a crucial role in optimizing performance. When running complex simulations, it is often beneficial to cache the simulation data to disk. This process involves storing the results of the simulation calculations so that you don't need to re-calculate them every time you make changes. In Blender, this is managed through the Cache section in the Physics Properties tab, where you can specify the location and size of the cache. Properly managing cache files can significantly speed up your workflow and prevent unnecessary reprocessing.

By mastering these various physics simulations—rigid bodies, fluids, and cloth—you can create more dynamic and visually engaging animations. Each simulation type requires a deep understanding of its settings and interactions, but with practice, you will be able to incorporate these elements seamlessly into your projects.

Physics Simulations

Building on the fundamentals of rigid body and fluid simulations, the next area of focus is cloth simulations, which provide another dimension of realism by simulating the behavior of fabrics. Cloth simulations in Blender allow you to create dynamic, natural-looking cloth movements, such as flowing garments or draping curtains. Setting up a cloth simulation involves a few key steps that ensure the fabric behaves as intended in your scene.

To start with, select the mesh object that you want to simulate as cloth. This mesh will act as your fabric, and it's crucial to ensure that it has a sufficient level of geometry to deform naturally. If the mesh is too low-poly, the resulting simulation may appear blocky or unrealistic. Once you have your cloth mesh ready, you need to assign cloth simulation properties to it by navigating to the Physics Properties tab and enabling the Cloth option.

The Cloth settings offer various parameters that influence how the fabric behaves under simulation. For instance, the "Quality" setting determines the simulation's resolution and accuracy. Increasing this value will yield more detailed and accurate simulations but may also slow down performance. Another critical parameter is the "Mass," which affects how heavy the fabric appears. Lighter fabrics will flutter and billow more than heavier ones. Adjusting the "Stiffness" settings controls how rigid or flexible the cloth is, influencing how it reacts to forces and collisions.

In addition to these basic settings, Blender provides options for defining how the cloth interacts with other objects in the scene. You can set up collision properties to ensure that the cloth properly collides with other meshes, such as a character's body or furniture. The "Collision" settings under the Physics Properties tab of the interacting objects need to be enabled, and parameters such as "Thickness" and "Damping" should be adjusted to refine the interaction.

Simulation Cache is another vital concept when working with cloth simulations. The cache stores the results of the simulation, which allows you to play back and review the animation without recalculating it every time. It is essential to bake the simulation cache before rendering, ensuring that all cloth movements are accurately captured and do not change during playback. To bake the cache, go to the "Cache" section within the Cloth settings and click the "Bake" button. This process may take some time depending on the complexity of the simulation and the hardware capabilities.

In addition to the core simulation types—rigid bodies, fluids, and cloths—Blender offers more specialized simulations, such as smoke and fire. These are particularly useful for creating effects that involve combustion or atmospheric interactions. The setup for smoke and fire simulations is similar to that of fluids: you start by defining a domain object and assigning the appropriate simulation properties. The domain object acts as the container for the smoke or fire effect, and the settings within the Smoke or Fire properties tab allow you to control the behavior of the effect.

Blender's smoke simulation is quite versatile, enabling you to create everything from subtle steam to explosive plumes. Key parameters include the "Smoke Density," which affects how thick the smoke appears, and the "Temperature Difference," which influences the rise and dispersion of the smoke. For fire simulations, you can control the "Flame Rate" and "Heat," adjusting how intense and persistent the fire is.

It's crucial to test and iterate your simulations to achieve the desired results. Given that physical simulations can be computationally expensive, it is often helpful to start with lower resolutions and gradually increase them as you refine the effect. This iterative approach allows you to balance realism with performance, ensuring that your final output is both visually compelling and computationally feasible.

Lastly, Blender's physics simulations can be combined to create complex effects. For example, you can simulate a scene where a cloth drapes over a rigid body that interacts with a fluid, such as a wet towel hanging on a rail. Combining different simulations requires careful coordination of settings and parameters to ensure that each simulation interacts naturally with the others. This approach often involves baking each simulation separately and then combining the results in your final render.

By mastering these physics simulations in Blender, you can significantly enhance the realism and dynamism of your animations. Each simulation type—rigid body, fluid, cloth, smoke, and fire—offers unique capabilities that, when used effectively, can transform a static scene into a vibrant, interactive experience.

Physics Simulations

Continuing with the exploration of Blender's physics engines, the next focus is on fluid simulations, which are essential for creating realistic water, smoke, and other liquid effects. Fluid simulations in Blender are powerful tools for achieving dynamic and visually compelling scenes that require fluid dynamics. The process begins with defining the fluid domain, setting up fluid objects, and configuring simulation parameters to control the behavior of the fluids.

To initiate a fluid simulation, you first need to create a domain object, which acts as the container for your fluid. The domain should encompass the entire area where you want the fluid to be simulated, ensuring that the fluid particles interact correctly within the boundaries. Create a mesh that will serve as your domain, and then apply the fluid simulation by navigating to the Physics Properties tab and selecting the Fluid option.

Within the Fluid settings, you must specify the type of fluid simulation you want: either as a fluid domain or a fluid object. The fluid domain controls the simulation area, while fluid objects, such as inflows, outflows, or obstacles, interact with the fluid within this domain. To designate an object as a fluid, set its type to either Fluid or Effector, depending on its role. For instance, an inflow object introduces fluid into the domain, while an outflow object removes it.

The fluid simulation parameters include several settings that influence how the fluid behaves. The "Resolution" setting is particularly crucial, as it determines the level of detail in the fluid simulation. Higher resolution values will result in more detailed fluid effects but require significantly more computational resources. Additionally, parameters such as "Viscosity" and "Surface Tension" help define the fluid's physical properties, affecting how it flows and interacts with surfaces.

Simulating fluid interactions can also involve complex behaviors, such as splashes, waves, or foam. To achieve these effects, Blender's fluid simulation system provides advanced options such as particle systems and mesh caching. Particle systems can be used to simulate small droplets or splashes that occur when fluids interact with other surfaces. Meanwhile, mesh caching allows you to store and replay simulation results, which can be useful for rendering complex fluid scenes efficiently.

For rigid body dynamics, the focus shifts to simulating solid objects that can collide, break, and interact with one another based on physical properties. Setting up rigid body simulations involves defining objects as either active or passive. Active objects are those that move and interact based on physics, while passive objects act as static elements in the scene. To configure a rigid body simulation, select the objects you wish to include and assign them the appropriate rigid body type in the Physics Properties tab.

Rigid body settings include parameters such as "Mass," "Friction," and "Bounciness," which influence how objects respond to forces and collisions. The "Mass" parameter determines how heavy an object is, affecting its movement and interaction with other objects. "Friction" controls how much resistance is encountered when objects slide against each other, while "Bounciness" adjusts how much an object rebounds after a collision.

When dealing with complex scenes involving many objects, constraint systems can be employed to control the relationships between different rigid bodies. Constraints such as hinges and springs allow for more sophisticated interactions and movement, enabling objects to behave in a more realistic manner based on the constraints you define.

Finally, integrating these various physics simulations into a coherent animation requires careful management of simulation caching and performance optimization. Simulations can be resource-intensive, and as such, it's important to bake the simulations and optimize settings to balance detail and performance. Baking is a process where Blender precomputes the physics calculations, storing the results for efficient playback and rendering. Proper optimization ensures that your simulations run smoothly without unnecessary computational overhead, allowing for a more efficient workflow and higher-quality final outputs.

In summary, mastering Blender's physics simulations involves a deep understanding of how to set up and manage rigid body dynamics, fluid simulations, and cloth simulations. By adjusting simulation parameters, employing constraints, and managing performance, you can create dynamic and realistic animations that enhance the visual impact of your scenes.

Rendering Basics

Rendering is a critical phase in the animation pipeline, converting the intricate 3D models and animations into final 2D images or sequences. It's essential to understand how to set up and configure the rendering process in Blender to achieve high-quality results. The process begins with selecting a render engine, configuring scene settings, and fine-tuning the output to match your desired quality and style.

To start, Blender offers several render engines, each with distinct features and advantages. The most commonly used render engines are Cycles and Eevee. Cycles is a physically-based path-tracer that simulates realistic lighting and materials, ideal for high-quality renders where realism is paramount. It handles complex lighting interactions, such as reflections and refractions, with precision. On the other hand, Eevee is a real-time render engine optimized for speed and interactive feedback. It uses screen-space effects and approximations to produce high-quality results quickly, making it suitable for real-time applications and faster previews.

Selecting the appropriate render engine is the first step in setting up your scene for rendering. To do this, navigate to the Render Properties tab in Blender and choose your preferred engine from the Render Engine dropdown menu. Each engine will have its own set of settings and optimizations, so familiarizing yourself with the options available for your chosen engine is crucial.

Next, configure the camera settings, which play a pivotal role in framing your shots and defining the perspective from which your scene will be rendered. Blender provides various camera properties, such as focal length, depth of field, and sensor size, which can be adjusted to achieve the desired effect. The focal length, for example, affects the field of view and perspective distortion, which can greatly influence the final appearance of your render. Depth of field can be used to create a realistic blur effect in the background or foreground, adding a sense of depth to your scene.

Once your camera is set up, you need to configure the lighting, which significantly impacts the look and feel of your render. Lighting in Blender can be controlled through different light sources, including point lights, spotlights, sun lamps, and area lights. Each type of light source has its unique properties and uses. For instance, point lights emit light in all directions from a single point, creating a spherical light distribution, while spotlights focus light in a cone shape, allowing for more controlled illumination. Sun lamps simulate sunlight with parallel rays, and area lights provide diffuse light with a soft, shadowless quality.

In addition to setting up lights, it's important to adjust the lighting settings in the Render Properties tab. Here, you can configure global illumination, shadow quality, and ambient occlusion. Global illumination affects how light bounces around the scene, contributing to the overall realism of the lighting. Shadow quality settings determine the resolution and softness of shadows cast by light sources. Ambient occlusion adds depth to scenes by darkening areas where objects are close together, enhancing the sense of volume and spatial relationships.

The next critical aspect is configuring the render settings, which includes choosing the output resolution, file format, and sampling rates. The output resolution determines the size and quality of your final images or animations. Higher resolutions will produce more detailed renders but require more computational power and time. Blender allows you to set the resolution in pixels and aspect ratio to fit different output requirements.

For file formats, Blender supports various options such as PNG, JPEG, TIFF, and EXR. PNG is commonly used for its lossless compression, preserving image quality, while JPEG offers smaller file sizes with lossy compression, suitable for web use. TIFF and EXR are used for high-quality images and are often utilized in professional workflows where preserving color accuracy and detail is critical.

Sampling rates are another crucial setting in the rendering process. In Cycles, the number of samples determines the quality of the render. Higher sampling rates reduce noise and produce cleaner images but increase rendering times. Eevee, on the other hand, uses screen-space reflections and other techniques to simulate high-quality effects more efficiently, though it may require adjustments to achieve the desired level of detail and realism.

Finally, once all settings are configured, you can proceed to render your scene. Blender offers various rendering options, including rendering a single frame, a range of frames, or an entire animation sequence. For animations, Blender can output individual frames as images or compile them into video files. Ensure that you set up the frame range and output directory correctly to manage your rendered assets effectively.

The rendering process can be resource-intensive, especially for complex scenes and high-resolution outputs. Monitoring performance and managing render times are essential for efficient workflows. By understanding and applying these rendering basics, you'll be well-equipped to produce high-quality visuals that bring your 3D creations to life.

When configuring lighting for rendering, the choice and placement of light sources are critical in achieving the desired effect. Point lights provide a natural, omnidirectional illumination but can create harsh shadows unless diffused. Spotlights focus light in a specific direction, allowing for controlled illumination and shadow casting. Sun lamps simulate sunlight, providing parallel light rays that can effectively mimic outdoor lighting scenarios. Area lights offer a more diffuse light source, ideal for creating soft shadows and evenly lit scenes. Each of these light types can be adjusted for intensity, color, and position to fit the needs of your scene.

In addition to configuring individual lights, the overall lighting setup can be enhanced by utilizing world settings, such as ambient light and environmental textures. Ambient light provides a base level of illumination across the entire scene, reducing harsh shadows and ensuring consistent light distribution. Environmental textures, such as HDRIs (High Dynamic Range Images), can be used to provide realistic lighting and reflections by simulating real-world environments.

Once the lighting is set, the next step involves configuring the render settings. These settings dictate how Blender processes the scene and generates the final output. In the Render Properties tab, you can adjust several critical settings, including resolution, frame rate, and render samples. Resolution determines the dimensions of the final image or animation, impacting both the level of detail and the file size. Higher resolutions yield more detailed renders but require more processing power and time. Frame rate controls the smoothness of animations, with standard rates being 24, 30, or 60 frames per second. Adjusting the render samples affects the quality of the final output—higher samples result in less noise and more accurate lighting but increase render times.

For rendering with Cycles, the number of samples plays a significant role in the quality of the final image. Higher sample counts reduce noise and improve the accuracy of light simulations but also increase render times. Blender allows you to preview your scene with a lower number of samples to assess composition and lighting before committing to a high-quality render.

In addition to render samples, other settings in Cycles, such as denoising, can help improve the final output. Denoising algorithms analyze the image and reduce visual noise, which is particularly useful in scenes with complex lighting or low sample counts. Blender provides built-in denoising options that can be enabled in the Render Properties tab, ensuring cleaner results without excessive render time.

For Eevee, the settings differ slightly but still include essential options such as shadow quality, ambient occlusion, and screen-space reflections. Eevee's real-time rendering approach requires efficient settings to balance visual quality and performance. Adjusting shadow settings, for example, can significantly impact the appearance of shadows in your scene, affecting both their sharpness and the performance of the render engine. Ambient occlusion adds depth to your scene by darkening areas where surfaces meet, while screen-space reflections enhance the realism of reflective surfaces.

When preparing for the final render, it is crucial to consider the output format and file settings. Blender supports various formats, including PNG, JPEG, and EXR, each suited for different purposes. PNG and JPEG are commonly used for images and are suitable for most general applications, while EXR is often used for high-dynamic-range images that retain more detail and color information.

To render an animation, you need to specify the frame range and output location in the Output Properties tab. Blender allows you to render a sequence of frames as an animation, which can be saved in formats such as AVI, MOV, or as an image sequence.

Rendering as an image sequence is beneficial for high-quality animations, as it allows you to edit individual frames or process them with compositing tools before creating the final video file.

Finally, during the rendering process, Blender provides a status bar that tracks the progress and estimated time remaining. Monitoring this progress helps you manage rendering times and make adjustments if needed. After the render is complete, review the output to ensure that all elements meet your expectations. If necessary, adjust the settings and re-render to achieve the desired results. By carefully configuring the render settings and understanding the impact of each option, you can produce high-quality images and animations that effectively showcase your 3D creations.

To ensure that your final render meets the desired quality, it's important to pay attention to the output settings within Blender. These settings determine the format, resolution, and destination of your rendered images or animations. In the Output Properties tab, you can specify the file format for your output, such as PNG, JPEG, or EXR for images, and formats like AVI, MP4, or MOV for animations. Each format has its own advantages: PNG supports transparency and lossless compression, while JPEG is useful for smaller file sizes with acceptable quality loss, and EXR is preferred for high dynamic range imaging.

Resolution settings are another crucial aspect. Higher resolutions provide more detail but also require more time and memory for rendering. When setting resolution, consider the final output medium—web, print, or video. For instance, standard HD video resolution is 1920x1080 pixels, while 4K resolution is 3840x2160 pixels. Blender also allows for custom resolution settings if specific dimensions are required.

When rendering animations, the choice of output settings affects not only the quality but also the efficiency of the rendering process. For animations, you can define the frame range and the output path where the rendered frames will be saved. If you are rendering a large animation, it is often useful to split the render into smaller segments or render in layers to manage memory usage and minimize the risk of crashes.

For more efficient rendering, consider utilizing Blender's built-in render engines: Cycles and Eevee. Cycles is a path-tracing render engine known for its photorealistic output, making it ideal for high-quality, realistic scenes. It calculates light paths more accurately, which improves the quality of reflections, refractions, and shadows. Eevee, on the other hand, is a real-time render engine optimized for speed and interactivity. It provides a good balance between quality and performance, making it suitable for quicker previews and less demanding final renders.

Additionally, Blender offers render farms and distributed rendering solutions to expedite the rendering process. Render farms are external services or setups that utilize multiple machines to render scenes in parallel. This can significantly reduce render times, especially for complex animations or high-resolution outputs. Distributed rendering within Blender allows you to use multiple computers on a local network to share the rendering load, improving efficiency and reducing the time required to complete the render.

When preparing for the final render, ensure that all aspects of the scene are properly configured. Double-check the scene's lighting, materials, and camera settings to confirm that they align with the intended visual style. Preview your render at a lower quality to detect any issues with composition or lighting before committing to a full-resolution render.

Post-processing is also an essential step to refine the final output. Blender provides compositing tools to adjust color balance, add effects, and correct any artifacts or issues that might have arisen during the rendering process. The

Compositing workspace in Blender allows you to use nodes to perform various adjustments, such as color grading, adding motion blur, or correcting exposure. This step helps enhance the visual quality and consistency of the final output.

Lastly, once the rendering process is complete, it's vital to review the final result thoroughly. Evaluate the rendered images or animations for any issues such as unexpected artifacts, incorrect lighting, or compositional flaws. If necessary, make adjustments to the scene, re-render, and re-evaluate until the desired quality is achieved.

Mastering the rendering process in Blender involves understanding the interplay between render settings, scene configuration, and output requirements. By carefully setting up your render engines, optimizing settings, and utilizing post-processing tools, you can produce high-quality renders that effectively showcase your 3D models and animations. As you gain more experience with Blender's rendering capabilities, you'll be able to achieve even more sophisticated results and bring your creative vision to life with greater precision and efficiency.

CHAPTER 12: RIGGING AND ARMATURES

Rigging is a crucial step in the animation pipeline, enabling the transformation of static 3D models into dynamic, movable entities. This process involves creating a skeletal structure —referred to as an armature—that acts as the underlying framework for your character or complex object. Understanding rigging and armature setup is foundational for achieving realistic and fluid animations, allowing for intricate movements and expressions.

To begin with rigging, the first task is to create an armature. An armature consists of bones that are used to manipulate the mesh of the character or object. In Blender, this is accomplished through the Armature object, which you can add from the Add menu. Once added, the armature will be represented by a series of bones arranged in a hierarchical structure. Each bone in the armature corresponds to a specific part of the character or object, allowing for precise control over its movements.

The bones in an armature are essential for defining the motion and deformation of the model. When creating bones, it's important to place them correctly within the mesh to match the intended anatomy or structure. This involves positioning bones at key joints and areas that will influence the model's movement. For example, in a humanoid character, bones would be placed in the arms, legs, spine, and head. Each bone should be aligned in a way that ensures natural articulation when animated.

After the bones are set up, the next step is to assign them to the mesh. This process is known as weight painting. Weight painting determines how each bone influences the vertices of the mesh. In Blender, this is done by selecting the mesh and then entering Weight Paint mode. Here, you can assign different weights to various parts of the mesh, which controls the extent to which each bone affects those parts. For instance, the weight painting on the arm should ensure that when the arm bone is moved, the vertices of the arm mesh follow smoothly and naturally.

Proper weight painting is crucial for achieving realistic deformations. If weights are not assigned correctly, the mesh can deform in unnatural ways when bones are moved, leading to distortions and visual glitches. Blender provides tools such as automatic weight assignment and various painting brushes to assist in this process. However, manual adjustments are often necessary to refine the weights and ensure that the mesh deforms correctly.

Constraints play a significant role in rigging by defining the limitations and relationships between different bones. Constraints can be used to control how bones interact with each other, such as setting limits on rotation or position. For instance, an IK (Inverse Kinematics) constraint can be applied to the arm to control the end effector's movement, allowing the rest of the arm to follow in a more intuitive manner. This is particularly useful for creating realistic limb movements, such as walking or reaching.

Another important aspect of rigging is creating control rigs, which provide a user-friendly interface for animators. Control rigs are sets of custom controls that make it easier to manipulate the armature. These controls often include sliders, dials, and other UI elements that abstract the underlying bones, allowing animators to pose and animate the character without directly interacting with the bones. Creating effective control rigs involves designing intuitive controls that align with the character's movements and behaviors.

To build a control rig, you start by creating custom objects, such as empty meshes or shapes, which act as control handles. These controls are then parented or constrained to the bones of the armature. For example, a control handle for the character's hand might be linked to the hand bone, allowing the animator to move the hand easily by manipulating the handle. The setup of these controls should be carefully planned to ensure that they provide precise and flexible control over the character's movements.

Rigging also involves testing and refining the armature to ensure that it functions correctly across various poses and animations. This includes checking the deformation of the mesh in different poses and adjusting weights and constraints as needed. Rigging is often an iterative process, requiring multiple adjustments and refinements to achieve the desired results. It is essential to test the rig extensively to identify and address any issues before moving on to the animation phase.

Overall, rigging and armature setup are foundational skills in character animation, enabling you to create dynamic and believable movements. By mastering these techniques, you establish the groundwork for creating lifelike animations and complex interactions, ensuring that your characters move and express themselves in a natural and compelling manner.

Once the initial bone structure is in place and weight painting is applied, the next step in rigging involves setting up constraints and controllers to manage how the bones interact and move. Constraints are rules applied to bones that control their behavior, such as limiting their rotation or defining how they influence other bones. They play a vital role in creating complex, realistic movements and ensuring that the rig functions as intended.

In Blender, constraints can be added through the Bone Constraints panel. For example, the Inverse Kinematics (IK) constraint is essential for animating limbs, as it allows for more natural movement by calculating the necessary bone rotations to achieve a desired end position. Applying an IK constraint to a chain of bones, such as an arm or leg, simplifies the animation process. Instead of manually adjusting each bone to achieve a specific pose, you can move a single end effector, and the IK system automatically adjusts the intermediate bones accordingly.

In addition to IK, other constraints such as Copy Location, Copy Rotation, and Limit Rotation are used to refine the rig. The Copy Location constraint can be employed to ensure that one bone follows the position of another, while the Copy Rotation constraint ensures that one bone matches the rotation of another. Limit Rotation constraints can restrict how far a bone can rotate, preventing unnatural twists and ensuring that movements remain within realistic ranges.

Controllers are another crucial aspect of rigging, providing an intuitive way to animate complex rigs. Controllers are custom objects or bones designed to drive the movement of the rig. For example, a control bone might be used to manipulate facial expressions, allowing animators to adjust the character's expressions through a simple interface rather than directly manipulating individual facial bones. Controllers are typically designed to be user-friendly, often shaped and positioned to match the intended animation tasks.

To set up controllers, you will create additional bones or objects that act as the control handles. These controllers are linked to the bones they are meant to control through constraints or parenting. For instance, a control bone for the character's hand might be parented to the hand bone, enabling the animator to move the control bone to animate the hand's position and rotation.

Another key component in rigging is the use of custom properties and drivers. Custom properties allow you to add additional controls to your rig, such as sliders for adjusting muscle strength or facial features. Drivers are expressions or scripts that link these properties to the movements of bones or other rig elements. For instance, a driver might link a slider that controls the character's smile to the rotation of facial bones, enabling smooth and coordinated expression changes.

As you build your rig, it's essential to test its functionality and make adjustments as needed. This involves creating various test animations to ensure that the rig behaves as expected. During testing, pay attention to how the mesh deforms and whether the bones and controllers interact properly. Look for any issues such as undesirable deformations or constraints that do not work as intended. Refining the rig based on these tests is crucial for ensuring that it will perform well during actual animation work.

Rigging also involves preparing the character or object for specific types of animations. For example, if your character is going to perform acrobatic movements, you may need to enhance the rig with additional controls for more complex actions. This could involve adding extra bones for better flexibility or creating specialized controllers for unique movements.

Ultimately, rigging and armature setup form the backbone of character animation, providing the structure and controls needed to bring your models to life. By carefully constructing and refining your rig, you set the stage for creating dynamic and believable animations. This foundation allows animators to focus on the creative aspects of their work, knowing that the technical setup supports the intended movements and expressions.

In summary, rigging and armatures are essential elements in animation, enabling the creation of movable and flexible characters and objects. Through the careful construction of bones, application of constraints, and setup of controllers, you can ensure that your rig performs well and supports realistic animations. Testing and refining the rig is crucial for achieving high-quality results and ensuring that the character moves naturally and convincingly. With a solid understanding of rigging principles and techniques, you are well-equipped to bring your 3D models to life and create compelling animations.

Once the armature and initial constraints are in place, the next phase in rigging involves fine-tuning and testing the rig to ensure that it behaves as expected during animation. This involves several detailed steps to refine the rig's performance and address any issues that might arise during animation.

One critical aspect to focus on is the adjustment of the weight painting. Weight painting ensures that the mesh deforms correctly with the underlying skeleton. This process involves painting weights onto the mesh to indicate how much influence each bone has on different parts of the mesh. Accurate weight painting is essential for achieving natural deformations, particularly around joints where complex bending occurs. If the weights are not painted correctly, you may encounter issues such as undesirable creases, stretching, or collapsing, which can significantly affect the quality of the animation.

Blender provides various tools to assist with weight painting. For example, the Weight Paint mode allows you to visualize how weights are distributed across the mesh using color gradients. Red typically represents full influence, while blue indicates minimal to no influence. Adjusting these weights can be done using brushes with different strengths and falloff settings to ensure smooth transitions and realistic deformations.

In addition to weight painting, it is crucial to test

the rig extensively to identify any potential issues. This includes animating the character through various poses and movements to observe how the mesh deforms and how the rig responds. Testing different animation scenarios can help uncover problems such as joint collapsing, bone intersections, or incorrect stretching. Regular testing allows you to make iterative adjustments and corrections, improving the rig's overall performance.

Another important consideration is the use of corrective shape keys, which are essential for addressing issues that arise during extreme deformations. Shape keys, also known as blend shapes or morph targets, are used to create corrective adjustments to the mesh during specific poses. For instance, when a character's elbow bends, you might use shape keys to adjust the mesh to avoid pinching or collapsing around the joint. This technique helps maintain realistic deformation and enhances the visual quality of the animation.

Creating user-friendly controls is another significant aspect of rigging. The rig should be designed with animators in mind, providing intuitive and accessible controls for all necessary movements and expressions. Custom control objects, such as sliders and buttons, can be created and linked to various rig components to streamline the animation process. For instance, facial rigs might include controls for adjusting eyebrow raises, mouth shapes, and eye movements, allowing animators to achieve precise expressions with ease.

Additionally, it is beneficial to implement a naming convention and organize the rig components systematically. A clear naming convention helps avoid confusion and ensures that all parts of the rig are easily identifiable. Proper organization of rig elements also contributes to a more efficient workflow, allowing for quicker adjustments and better management of complex rigs.

Lastly, documenting the rigging process and creating a user guide for the rig can be invaluable. This documentation should include detailed explanations of the rig's features, control descriptions, and any specific instructions for using the rig effectively. Providing clear guidance ensures that anyone using the rig, whether it be yourself or another animator, can understand and utilize it to its fullest potential.

In summary, the process of rigging and configuring armatures involves several crucial steps to ensure that the rig functions correctly and meets the needs of the animation. This includes setting up constraints, creating intuitive controllers, refining weight painting, testing the rig, and incorporating corrective shape keys. By focusing on these aspects, you create a robust and flexible rig that enables dynamic and realistic animations. Proper documentation and organization further enhance the usability and efficiency of the rig, setting the foundation for high-quality animation work.

CHAPTER 13:
SKINNING AND
WEIGHT PAINTING

In the domain of 3D animation, skinning and weight painting are pivotal processes that ensure your model deforms in a realistic manner when animated. After setting up the rigging for your character, the next step is to bind the mesh to the armature, which involves skinning. Skinning is the process of associating the mesh with the armature's bones, allowing the mesh to move and deform in harmony with the underlying skeleton. This binding is essential for achieving believable character animations, as it dictates how the mesh responds to the movement of the bones.

The first task in this process is to ensure that the mesh is properly assigned to the armature. This involves creating a vertex group for each bone in the armature. Each vertex group will correspond to a specific bone, allowing you to define how much influence that bone has on different parts of the mesh. In Blender, this is achieved through the Vertex Groups panel, where you can manually assign vertices to the appropriate groups. The accuracy of this assignment is critical; incorrect assignments can lead to unnatural deformations or animation glitches.

Once the vertex groups are set up, the next step is to perform weight painting. Weight painting is a technique used to fine-tune the influence of each bone on the mesh. It involves painting weights onto the vertices of the mesh, with each weight value representing the extent of influence a particular bone has over the vertex. In Blender, this is done in Weight Paint mode, where you can see a visual representation of the weights applied to the mesh, typically displayed as a gradient from red (full influence) to blue (no influence).

To achieve smooth and realistic deformations, it is essential to carefully paint the weights. Begin by painting weights in areas that will experience significant movement or deformation, such as joints. The goal is to ensure that the mesh deforms naturally as the bones move. For example, when a character's arm bends, the weight distribution around the elbow should allow for smooth bending without causing noticeable stretching or collapsing.

Several tools and techniques in Blender can assist with this process. The Weight Paint tool provides various brushes and settings that allow for precise weight adjustments. The "Add" and "Subtract" brushes enable you to increase or decrease weights on specific areas. The "Blur" brush helps smooth out weight transitions between different areas, reducing harsh lines and creating more natural deformations. It is also beneficial to use the "Normalize All" option, which ensures that the sum of all weights for each vertex equals 1, preventing any imbalances in the mesh deformation.

Fine-tuning the weight painting often involves iterative adjustments. After making initial weight adjustments, it is crucial to test the mesh by posing the rig and observing how the mesh deforms. This step helps identify any areas where the weights might be causing undesirable effects, such as pinching or stretching. You can then go back and adjust the weights as needed to address these issues. Testing different poses and movements will help you achieve more accurate and lifelike deformations.

In addition to manual weight painting, Blender offers automated tools that can assist in the skinning process. For instance, the "Automatic Weights" option in the Armature modifier automatically assigns weights based on the bone's proximity to the mesh. While this can provide a good starting point, it often requires manual refinement to achieve optimal results.

Corrective shape keys can also play a significant role in enhancing the quality of the skinning. Shape keys, or blend shapes, allow you to create specific adjustments to the mesh during extreme deformations. For example, when a character's knee bends, shape keys can be used to correct any undesirable deformation that occurs around the knee joint, such as bulging or collapsing. These adjustments help maintain a more realistic appearance and improve the overall quality of the animation.

Lastly, when working on weight painting, it is essential to pay attention to the overall topology of the mesh. Properly structured topology, with evenly distributed vertices and well-defined edge loops, can greatly affect how the mesh deforms. A well-structured mesh will facilitate more accurate weight painting and lead to smoother deformations during animation.

By mastering the techniques of skinning and weight painting, you ensure that your 3D models will move and deform naturally in your animations. This foundational work is crucial for achieving high-quality, lifelike animations that convincingly convey movement and emotion. The attention to detail in this stage of the animation pipeline lays the groundwork for creating dynamic and engaging animated characters.

Continuing with skinning and weight painting, let us delve deeper into the specifics of the weight painting process. A critical aspect to address is the balance of weight distribution across the mesh. Proper weight distribution ensures that the deformations are not only smooth but also natural, mimicking real-life physics and anatomical movement.

When working with weight painting in Blender, it's essential to understand the concept of weight normalization. Each vertex in the mesh must be influenced by the bones it is associated with, and the sum of these influences must be equal to one. This means that if a vertex is influenced by multiple bones, the weights for these bones should collectively sum up to one, ensuring that the deformation is accurately represented. This principle helps prevent problems such as vertices pulling excessively or not moving in accordance with the rig.

One effective method to manage weight distribution is using the "Automatic Weights" feature during the initial binding of the mesh to the armature. This automatic process provides a starting point, applying weights based on proximity and the mesh's geometry relative to the bones. While this automatic process is useful, it often requires manual adjustment to fine-tune the weights and correct any issues, such as areas with excessive stretching or compression.

As you proceed with manual weight painting, pay attention to areas of the mesh that deform irregularly. Common problem areas include joints and extremities where the mesh may fold or stretch. For example, in a character's elbow or knee, you need to ensure that the weight distribution allows for a smooth, natural bend. To correct issues in these areas, use the "Add" and "Subtract" brushes strategically. Start with larger brush sizes to cover broader areas and gradually switch to smaller brushes for detailed adjustments.

The "Blur" brush is also indispensable for smoothing out weight transitions. Often, abrupt changes in weight can lead to visible artifacts in the deformation. By using the Blur brush, you can soften these transitions, ensuring a more fluid and natural deformation. Additionally, employing the "Normalize All" function can be beneficial, as it automatically adjusts the weights so that their total is normalized to one, helping to eliminate any inconsistencies.

For more complex meshes or those with intricate details, Blender offers advanced tools such as the "Vertex Weight Proximity" and "Vertex Weight Edit" modifiers. These tools provide additional control over how weights are applied based on various criteria, such as proximity to other objects or vertex positions. They can be especially useful for fine-tuning weight distributions in large, detailed models where manual weight painting might be cumbersome.

Moreover, it is crucial to regularly test the rig during the weight painting process. Testing involves posing the character in various positions and animations to observe how the mesh deforms in response to the rig's movements. This iterative testing and refinement process helps identify any areas that require adjustment, ensuring that the final animation will be smooth and natural.

Another important consideration in weight painting is the impact of different types of bones on the mesh. For instance, if your rig includes control bones or helper bones, ensure that their influence is properly managed to avoid unintended deformations. Control bones are often used for more specific adjustments or to influence secondary deformations, and their weight influence should be balanced carefully to achieve the desired effect.

As you refine your weight painting, it's beneficial to work with multiple views and reference images. Having a clear view of the mesh from different angles allows you to detect and correct issues that may not be apparent in a single view. Reference images, particularly those showing the mesh in various poses or animations, can help guide your weight painting efforts, ensuring that the final result aligns with your intended design and movement.

In summary, mastering skinning and weight painting is integral to creating realistic and fluid animations. By carefully managing weight distributions, employing Blender's advanced tools, and conducting iterative testing, you can ensure that your character or object deforms naturally during animation. This meticulous approach not only enhances the visual quality of your animations but also contributes to a more dynamic and lifelike representation of movement.

To ensure your model deforms correctly during animation, the precision of skinning and weight painting is paramount. Having addressed the fundamental principles and techniques of weight painting, it's essential to explore how these elements are applied practically to enhance the realism and functionality of your animations.

Firstly, let's discuss the intricacies of painting weights on a complex mesh. When dealing with models that have multiple overlapping bone influences, like those seen in characters with high levels of detail or complex clothing, fine control is necessary. Here, the weight painting tools in Blender become crucial. For instance, the "Weight Paint" mode provides a visual representation of weight distribution across your model. By painting directly onto the mesh, you can see how different areas are influenced by the bones, which helps in identifying and correcting deformation issues in real time.

The painting tools allow for different brush settings, such as strength and radius, to be adjusted according to the specific needs of the mesh. For more granular control, use the "Vertex Groups" panel to directly modify the weights assigned to specific bone groups. This panel is instrumental when you need to adjust weights without affecting other areas of the mesh. In conjunction with this, the "Vertex Weight Proximity" modifier can be used to dynamically adjust weights based on the distance between vertices and a target object, offering another layer of precision for complex deformations.

Attention to specific anatomical areas, like the shoulders and hips, requires careful manipulation of weights. For example, when animating arm movements, it's crucial that the shoulder area deforms smoothly to avoid unnatural stretching or pinching. Adjusting weights in these areas ensures that the mesh conforms realistically to the underlying bone structure, maintaining both visual fidelity and functional integrity.

In addition to manual weight painting, Blender provides several automated tools that can assist in refining the skinning process. The "Smooth" function, found in the Weight Paint toolset, can be used to even out weight distributions, which is particularly useful for eliminating jagged edges or abrupt changes in influence. Similarly, the "Average" function can balance the weights among a set of selected vertices, ensuring that no single vertex is disproportionately influenced by a particular bone.

For character models that include clothing or accessories, it's essential to manage weight painting on these elements carefully. Clothing should be weighted to the bones of the character, but also must retain its shape and appearance throughout various movements. Using the "Pin" feature during weight painting helps in preserving the intended shape of garments or accessories, allowing them to move naturally with the character while maintaining their original design.

When preparing for animation, always test your weight painting by creating various poses and animations. This practical approach allows you to observe how the mesh deforms in different scenarios, highlighting any areas where adjustments are needed. It's advisable to use a range of test animations, from basic poses to complex movements, to ensure that your skinning holds up under different conditions.

Finally, keep in mind that weight painting is often an iterative process. You might need to revisit and refine the weights multiple times, especially when working with complex rigs or high-detail models. Regularly checking your animations and deformations during this process will help you identify and correct issues early, leading to more polished and professional results.

In summary, mastering skinning and weight painting is crucial for achieving realistic and dynamic character animations. By applying the techniques outlined, including meticulous weight adjustments, leveraging Blender's advanced tools, and continually testing your models, you'll be well-equipped to create lifelike animations that accurately reflect the underlying rig and skeletal structure.

CHAPTER 14:
ANIMATION BASICS

In the realm of 3D animation, bringing static models to life requires a thorough understanding of fundamental animation principles. The essence of animation lies in creating the illusion of movement through the manipulation of keyframes and timelines. To initiate the animation process in Blender, it is essential to grasp these core concepts and tools.

To begin, the concept of keyframing is central to defining animation. Keyframes are markers that denote specific points in time where a change occurs in your object's properties, such as position, rotation, or scale. When setting up a basic animation, you start by selecting an object in your scene that you wish to animate. In Blender, you will first position your object in its starting pose or state, then insert a keyframe to mark this moment. This is achieved by pressing the 'I' key, which brings up the keyframe menu where you can select the property you wish to animate, such as location, rotation, or scale.

As you proceed, move the timeline cursor to a new frame where you want the next change to occur. Adjust the object to its new position or state and insert another keyframe. Blender will automatically interpolate the movement between these keyframes, creating a smooth transition from one state to another. This process is fundamental for animating both objects and characters.

The timeline in Blender is your primary tool for managing

these keyframes. It allows you to see and edit the sequence of events over time. The timeline interface displays a horizontal bar representing the animation's duration, with frames laid out along it. You can drag the playhead to different points in time to preview how the animation unfolds. For more advanced control, the Dope Sheet and Graph Editor are invaluable tools. The Dope Sheet provides a simplified view of all the keyframes and allows you to move and adjust them across different properties. The Graph Editor, on the other hand, offers a detailed view of animation curves, letting you fine-tune the motion by editing the F-Curves that represent changes in value over time.

The animation workspace in Blender is specifically designed to streamline the animation process. It is divided into several panels, including the Timeline, Dope Sheet, and Graph Editor. Each panel serves a unique purpose, from laying out keyframes to visualizing and adjusting animation curves. Understanding how to navigate and use these panels effectively is crucial for creating fluid and natural animations.

When animating objects, it is often helpful to employ Blender's built-in interpolation methods. These methods determine how the software calculates the in-between frames based on your keyframes. By default, Blender uses Bezier interpolation, which creates smooth, curved transitions. However, for more control over the animation's pacing, you can choose from other types of interpolation, such as Linear or Constant. Linear interpolation produces a constant speed between keyframes, while Constant interpolation results in an abrupt change, with no interpolation between keyframes.

Another important aspect of animation is easing, which refers to the gradual acceleration and deceleration of movement. Easing helps create more natural and realistic animations by simulating the way objects and characters typically move in the real world. In Blender, you can adjust easing through the Graph Editor by manipulating the handles of the Bezier curves. These curves represent the speed and flow of your animation, and by modifying them, you can achieve a variety of effects, from a slow start and fast end to a smooth, continuous motion.

For animating characters, additional considerations are required. Once your character is rigged and the basic animation setup is complete, you will need to adjust the poses and movements to ensure they look natural. This involves keyframing not only the position of the character but also its limbs, facial expressions, and any other body parts that contribute to the animation. Utilizing Blender's pose libraries and action editor can streamline this process by allowing you to save and reuse different poses and animation sequences.

In essence, the process of animating in Blender involves setting keyframes to define important moments in the animation, utilizing the timeline and animation workspace to manage these keyframes, and applying interpolation and easing to create smooth, realistic movements. By mastering these basics, you will lay a strong foundation for more advanced animation techniques and achieve more compelling and lifelike results in your projects.

To effectively create animations in Blender, it is imperative to understand the principles that govern smooth and natural movement. Beyond simply placing keyframes, achieving fluid motion involves an understanding of interpolation and easing. When you set keyframes in Blender, the software uses interpolation to determine the intermediate frames between keyframes. By default, Blender uses linear interpolation, which creates a constant speed between keyframes. This might not always yield the most natural motion, as real-world movements often involve acceleration and deceleration.

To enhance the realism of your animations, you can utilize easing techniques. Easing controls how the animation speeds up or slows down as it transitions between keyframes. Blender provides several easing options, including ease-in, ease-out, and ease-in-out. Ease-in makes the animation start slowly and then speed up, while ease-out causes it to slow down towards the end. Ease-in-out combines both effects, giving the animation a more natural start and finish. You can adjust these settings in the Graph Editor by selecting keyframes and modifying the handle types to create the desired easing effect.

When animating complex movements, such as those involving characters, it is crucial to pay attention to timing and spacing. Timing refers to the speed of the animation, while spacing determines the distance between keyframes. Proper timing ensures that the movement feels right, whether it's a fast action like a jump or a slow action like a character turning their head. Spacing impacts how the object or character moves through the scene, affecting the perception of weight and realism. By adjusting the keyframe intervals and observing how the animation plays out, you can fine-tune these aspects to achieve the desired result.

In addition to keyframing and easing, another important technique is the use of secondary actions. Secondary actions are subtle movements that occur simultaneously with the primary action, adding depth and realism to the animation. For example, when a character walks, their arms should swing naturally. Similarly, when a character jumps, their hair or clothing might flutter. These secondary actions help to make the animation feel more lifelike and can be achieved by adding additional keyframes and adjusting the timing and spacing of these movements.

Blender's animation tools also offer functionality for dealing with more advanced animation techniques, such as rigging and inverse kinematics. Rigging, as previously discussed, involves creating a skeleton for characters or objects, which allows for more complex and realistic movements. Inverse kinematics (IK) is a technique used to automatically adjust the position of a limb or body part based on the position of another part. For instance, when animating a character walking, IK can be used to ensure that the character's feet stay planted on the ground as the body moves.

The Animation workspace in Blender is designed to integrate these various tools and techniques, providing a comprehensive environment for animating your models. The workspace includes panels and editors tailored for animation tasks, such as the Timeline for managing keyframes, the Dope Sheet for arranging and editing keyframes, and the Graph Editor for refining animation curves. Each of these components plays a critical role in creating and fine-tuning animations, allowing you to achieve precise and polished results.

As you become more familiar with Blender's animation tools and techniques, you will find that practice and experimentation are key to mastering the art of animation. Continuously refining your animations by adjusting keyframes, easing, timing, and secondary actions will lead to more compelling and believable results. Whether you are animating a simple object or a complex character, the principles and practices outlined here will provide a solid foundation for creating dynamic and engaging animations.

To ensure that animations convey a sense of life and authenticity, it is crucial to master the principles of animation in depth. This includes a thorough understanding of the animation workspace, keyframes, and the various tools Blender provides for refining motion.

The animation workspace in Blender is where much of the magic happens. It is divided into several key panels: the Timeline, the Graph Editor, and the Dope Sheet. The Timeline is where you manage the overall sequence of your animation. It displays the frame numbers along with the duration of your animation. Here, you can scrub through the timeline to preview your animation or set specific frames to add keyframes.

The Dope Sheet is a powerful tool for managing keyframes. It provides a more detailed view of keyframes across different objects and actions. This sheet allows you to select, move, and adjust keyframes to refine the timing of your animation. For instance, if you notice that a character's arm movement starts too abruptly, you can adjust the keyframes in the Dope Sheet to smooth out the motion.

The Graph Editor offers a visual representation of the animation curves associated with your keyframes. These curves display how the properties of your objects, such as location, rotation, and scale, change over time. By adjusting these curves, you can create more nuanced and realistic animations. For instance, easing curves can be adjusted to create more natural acceleration and deceleration. The Graph Editor's ability to fine-tune these curves allows you to control the velocity of your animation with great precision.

Blender also provides various tools and techniques for refining your animations beyond basic keyframing. One such tool is the use of motion paths. Motion paths show the trajectory of your animated objects over time, which can be extremely useful for visualizing and correcting complex movements. By enabling motion paths in the viewport, you can observe how an object moves through space and make adjustments as necessary.

Another advanced feature is the use of Animation Layers. This allows you to create and manage multiple layers of animation on top of each other. For instance, you might have a base animation layer for a character's walk cycle and an additional layer for facial expressions. This separation helps in making adjustments and refinements to specific aspects of the animation without affecting the entire sequence.

When animating characters, it is important to consider the principles of weight and physicality. Realistic movement often involves understanding the weight distribution and the impact of actions on different parts of the body. For example, a character lifting an object should exhibit a shift in posture and weight as the object's mass affects their balance. To capture these nuances, you might need to add keyframes for subtle body adjustments, ensuring that the character's movement looks natural and convincing.

The interpolation types available in Blender also play a crucial role in refining animations. While linear interpolation provides a constant motion between keyframes, Bezier interpolation allows for more natural easing in and out. By adjusting the handles of Bezier curves in the Graph Editor, you can create smooth transitions between keyframes, enhancing the overall fluidity of your animation.

To further polish your animations, consider the use of animation retargeting. This technique involves transferring animations from one character to another, which can be particularly useful when working with multiple characters or when reusing animations. Blender's retargeting tools allow you to map the animation data from one rig to another, making it easier to maintain consistency across different models.

As you progress in your animation skills, you will likely encounter the need to animate complex interactions between objects and characters. This involves setting up interactions that are not just visually appealing but also physically plausible. For example, animating a character interacting with a dynamic object, such as a ball, requires careful consideration of the object's movement and how it responds to the character's actions. Using Blender's physics simulations in tandem with keyframing can help achieve more realistic results.

Mastering the basics of animation is essential for creating compelling and lifelike movements. By understanding the principles of keyframing, easing, timing, and the various tools within Blender, you can develop animations that not only bring your models to life but also enhance the storytelling of your projects. The ability to create smooth, natural motion is a foundational skill that will greatly contribute to the quality and impact of your animations.

Advanced Animation Techniques

Building on the foundational concepts of animation, we now delve into more sophisticated techniques that enhance the control and precision of your animations. These techniques involve intricate keyframing, nuanced curve editing, and advanced tools such as the Dope Sheet and Action Editor. Mastery of these elements will enable you to handle complex animation projects with greater finesse and detail.

To begin with, complex keyframing involves a deeper understanding of how keyframes interact with each other across different frames. While basic keyframing allows you to set key positions and motions at specific points in time, advanced keyframing requires careful manipulation of these keyframes to achieve smoother and more fluid animations. This often involves setting additional keyframes to fine-tune the timing and transition between different poses or actions. For example, animating a character jumping might require keyframes for the start, peak, and landing of the jump, but it also involves intermediary keyframes to adjust the arc and speed of the jump for a more natural motion.

Curve editing is an essential skill in refining the motion of your animations. The Graph Editor provides a visual representation of the animation curves associated with your keyframes. These curves reflect how properties such as position, rotation, and scale change over time. By manipulating these curves, you can control the acceleration and deceleration of your animation, making movements appear more lifelike. For instance, adjusting the ease-in and ease-out of a curve can make an object's motion start and stop more smoothly, avoiding abrupt or unnatural transitions.

The Graph Editor also allows you to work with F-Curves, which are functions that define the trajectory of your animations. Understanding how to adjust these curves is crucial for achieving precise control over motion. You can use tools within the Graph Editor to smooth out irregularities in the curves or to create complex animations with multiple overlapping motions. For instance, if an object is rotating while moving along a path, you would need to adjust both the location and rotation curves to ensure they synchronize correctly and appear seamless.

The Dope Sheet and Action Editor are additional powerful tools for managing animations. The Dope Sheet provides a broader view of keyframes across multiple objects and actions. It allows you to select and edit keyframes quickly, making it easier to adjust timing and synchronization. For instance, if you have multiple characters interacting in a scene, the Dope Sheet lets you view and manage their keyframes simultaneously, ensuring that their actions are coordinated effectively.

The Action Editor, on the other hand, is specifically designed for managing complex animations and creating reusable animation clips. It allows you to create, modify, and blend different actions, such as walking, running, or idle states, and then apply them to your characters. This feature is particularly useful when working on projects that require consistent animations across multiple scenes or characters. By creating and managing actions in the Action Editor, you can streamline your workflow and ensure that your animations remain coherent and fluid.

In addition to these tools, it is important to consider the role of advanced techniques such as motion capture data integration and procedural animation. Motion capture data can provide highly realistic movement by recording the actions of live actors and applying this data to your 3D models. Integrating motion capture with your animations involves importing and retargeting the captured data to match the rig of your character.

This technique is particularly useful for achieving complex and nuanced movements that might be difficult to animate manually.

Procedural animation, on the other hand, involves creating animations through algorithms and simulations rather than manually keyframing each movement. This technique is often used for generating natural and dynamic movements in response to changing conditions or interactions. For example, procedural animation can be used to simulate realistic cloth movement or character reactions based on environmental factors, providing a level of detail and realism that can enhance your animations significantly.

Mastering these advanced animation techniques requires practice and a deep understanding of how different elements of animation interact with each other. By becoming proficient with complex keyframing, curve editing, and the use of advanced tools like the Dope Sheet and Action Editor, you will be well-equipped to tackle intricate animation projects with greater control and precision.

Continuing from the previous exploration of complex keyframing and curve editing, we now turn our attention to the advanced tools that further refine and manage your animations: the Dope Sheet and Action Editor. These tools are invaluable for organizing and streamlining the animation process, particularly when dealing with intricate projects involving multiple characters or complex scenes.

The Dope Sheet offers a comprehensive overview of keyframes across different actions and objects. This tool provides a timeline view where you can see and manipulate keyframes for all animated properties in one place. Unlike the Graph Editor, which focuses on the interpolation of values over time, the Dope Sheet allows for more straightforward adjustments to keyframe placement. It's particularly useful for aligning actions between different objects or characters. For example, if you have a scene where a character is interacting with a prop, the Dope Sheet enables you to synchronize their movements by adjusting keyframes across both the character and the prop simultaneously. You can also easily copy, paste, or delete keyframes, which can expedite the animation process and ensure consistency.

In conjunction with the Dope Sheet, the Action Editor enhances your ability to manage multiple animations or "actions." Each action in the Action Editor represents a distinct set of keyframes for a particular animation, such as walking, jumping, or idle states. By creating separate actions, you can organize complex animations into manageable segments. For example, if you are animating a character who needs to perform a series of different actions throughout a scene, you can create separate actions for each behavior and then blend or transition between them as needed. This segmentation not only helps in keeping your animation project organized but also facilitates more detailed adjustments to individual actions without affecting others.

The Action Editor also supports the creation of action strips, which are segments of animation that can be blended or layered. This functionality is particularly useful when combining different actions, such as a character walking while carrying an object. By layering actions, you can maintain the integrity of each motion while ensuring that they work together seamlessly. For instance, if the character's walking animation needs to blend with a specific arm movement, the Action Editor allows you to create a smooth transition between these actions, ensuring that the final result looks cohesive and natural.

Moreover, understanding how to use NLA (Non-Linear Animation) strips in Blender can significantly enhance your workflow. The NLA Editor allows you to layer and blend multiple actions, offering a more flexible approach to animation. By utilizing NLA strips, you can create complex animations by combining different actions in a non-linear manner. This is particularly advantageous for animating characters with a wide range of behaviors or for scenes that require intricate choreography. For instance, a character might need to perform a series of actions such as walking, jumping, and interacting with objects. Using NLA strips, you can sequence these actions, adjust their timing, and create seamless transitions between them.

As you become more proficient with these advanced animation tools, you will find that your ability to manage and refine animations becomes more efficient and precise. Mastering the Dope Sheet, Action Editor, and NLA strips provides you with the tools to handle complex animations with greater control, ensuring that your animations are not only visually compelling but also functionally accurate.

In summary, advanced animation techniques in Blender involve a deep understanding of keyframing, curve editing, and the effective use of tools such as the Dope Sheet, Action Editor, and NLA strips. By integrating these techniques into your workflow, you can achieve a higher level of animation precision and creativity. These tools enable you to create fluid, realistic movements and manage complex animation sequences, ultimately enhancing the quality and depth of your animated projects.

To further refine your animations and achieve more complex results, mastering the principles of interpolation and easing curves is essential. The Graph Editor, as previously discussed, plays a pivotal role in this aspect. It allows you to manipulate the interpolation curves that dictate how smoothly an object's motion transitions between keyframes. By adjusting these curves, you can create more natural and fluid movements, enhancing the realism of your animation.

In the Graph Editor, you'll work primarily with bezier curves to control the acceleration and deceleration of movements. Bezier handles, which extend from the keyframes, adjust the rate at which the animation speeds up or slows down. For instance, to create a more lifelike walking animation, you might use an "ease-in" and "ease-out" approach. This means that the character's movement starts slowly, accelerates, and then slows down again as it comes to a stop. By tweaking the bezier handles, you can ensure that these transitions are smooth and realistic, avoiding any abrupt changes in speed that could disrupt the flow of the animation.

Moreover, the Graph Editor enables the creation of complex animation cycles by allowing for precise adjustments to individual curve segments. For example, if you are animating a character's arm swinging, you might need to fine-tune the arm's movement to ensure it follows a natural arc. By adjusting the curves in the Graph Editor, you can refine the motion so that it accurately reflects the physics of the arm swing, taking into account gravity and momentum.

The Dope Sheet and Action Editor, while excellent for managing and organizing animations, also integrate seamlessly with the Graph Editor. After adjusting keyframes and creating actions, you can use the Graph Editor to fine-tune the details of each action, ensuring that transitions between actions are smooth. This is particularly useful in scenarios where characters perform complex sequences involving multiple motions, such as a combination of walking, jumping, and interacting with objects. The ability to refine each action individually and then blend them effectively allows for greater control and a more polished final product.

Additionally, incorporating advanced techniques like constraints and drivers into your animations can add another layer of sophistication. Constraints allow you to control the movement of one object based on the properties of another, which is useful for creating complex interactions between characters and objects. For example, you might use a "Copy Location" constraint to ensure that a character's hand follows a specific path or an object maintains a consistent position relative to another. Drivers, on the other hand, enable you to link properties of one object to another using mathematical expressions. This can be particularly useful for automating repetitive tasks or ensuring consistent behavior across multiple objects.

As you work with constraints and drivers, it's important to test and adjust your animations frequently. By previewing your animations in real-time, you can identify any issues with movement or interaction and make adjustments as necessary. This iterative process helps to ensure that all elements of your animation work together harmoniously and achieve the desired result.

Finally, understanding the principles of animation, such as anticipation, follow-through, and secondary actions, is crucial for creating more dynamic and engaging animations. Anticipation involves preparing the audience for an upcoming action, such as a character crouching before jumping. Follow-through refers to the natural continuation of motion after the main action, like a character's hair or clothing continuing to move after they have stopped. Secondary actions add depth and realism to animations by introducing additional movements that complement the primary action, such as a character's hands or facial expressions reacting to their movements.

By applying these advanced animation techniques and principles, you'll be able to create more intricate and compelling animations. Mastery of keyframing, curve editing, and the effective use of animation tools such as the Graph Editor, Dope Sheet, and Action Editor will provide you with the control and precision needed to handle complex animation projects. This skill set is invaluable for animators seeking to push the boundaries of their craft and produce high-quality, lifelike animations that captivate and engage audiences.

CHAPTER 16: PHYSICS AND SIMULATIONS

Incorporating physics and simulations into your animations can significantly enhance their realism by replicating natural phenomena. Blender offers a variety of tools to achieve this, including rigid body dynamics, fluid simulations, and cloth simulations. Understanding and effectively utilizing these tools will elevate your ability to create dynamic and engaging animations.

Starting with rigid body dynamics, this tool is fundamental for simulating the behavior of solid objects when they collide or interact with one another. To set up a basic rigid body simulation in Blender, you first need to select the objects you want to include in the simulation. Once selected, navigate to the Physics Properties tab and enable the Rigid Body option. This action assigns physical properties to the objects, such as mass and friction, and determines how they will react to forces and collisions.

Rigid body dynamics are essential for simulating realistic interactions between objects, such as a stack of blocks falling over or a ball bouncing off a surface. The parameters you adjust, including mass, friction, and restitution (bounciness), directly affect the outcome of the simulation. For instance, increasing the friction value between two colliding objects will result in less sliding and more realistic contact. Similarly, adjusting the restitution value will control how much energy is retained or lost during impacts, influencing how bouncy or elastic the objects appear.

In addition to setting up rigid bodies, Blender provides tools for controlling simulations through constraints and forces. Constraints, such as hinges and springs, can be applied to objects to limit their movement and create specific types of interactions. For example, a hinge constraint allows an object to rotate around a fixed point, mimicking the behavior of a door or a pendulum. Forces like gravity, wind, and turbulence can also be applied to influence the motion of objects, adding further layers of complexity to the simulation.

Fluid simulations in Blender enable you to create realistic liquid effects, such as flowing water or pouring beverages. To start a fluid simulation, you'll first need to set up a domain, which is the volume within which the fluid simulation occurs. This domain object defines the boundaries of the simulation and will contain the fluid's interactions. Next, add a fluid object, which can be a mesh representing the liquid. This object is assigned the fluid type in the Physics Properties tab, where you can specify whether it should act as a liquid or gas.

Blender's fluid simulation system requires careful setup of several parameters to achieve realistic results. You'll need to define the resolution of the fluid domain, which affects the simulation's detail level. Higher resolutions result in more accurate simulations but require more computational power. Additionally, you can adjust the fluid's viscosity and surface tension to simulate different types of liquids, from thick syrups to thin water.

Once the simulation is set up, you can bake the fluid simulation to calculate and store the results. Baking is a crucial step, as it ensures that the simulation runs smoothly and consistently during playback. After baking, you can preview and render the fluid animation to see how the liquid behaves and interacts with other objects in the scene.

Cloth simulations in Blender are another powerful tool for creating realistic animations involving fabric and soft materials. To use cloth simulations, select the mesh that will act as the cloth and enable the Cloth option in the Physics Properties tab. This action assigns the necessary physical properties to the mesh, allowing it to behave like a piece of fabric that responds to forces, gravity, and interactions with other objects.

In the Cloth settings, you can adjust parameters such as mass, stiffness, and damping to control how the cloth reacts to movement and external forces. For example, increasing the stiffness will make the cloth less likely to fold or stretch, while a higher damping value will reduce the cloth's tendency to oscillate or flutter excessively. Additionally, you can define collision settings to prevent the cloth from passing through other objects and ensure that it interacts realistically with the environment.

The cloth simulation also requires baking to calculate the fabric's behavior over time. Once baked, you can animate the cloth by moving objects or applying forces, and the simulation will respond accordingly. This feature is particularly useful for animating characters wearing clothes or for creating effects such as flags waving in the wind.

In summary, mastering Blender's physics and simulation tools involves understanding and controlling how rigid bodies, fluids, and cloths interact within your scenes. By setting up and fine-tuning these simulations, you can create animations that are not only visually compelling but also imbued with a sense of realism that enhances the overall impact of your projects. Whether you are animating a cascading waterfall, a tumbling stack of blocks, or a billowing flag, these tools provide the means to bring dynamic and engaging effects to life.

Continuing with fluid simulations, once the domain and fluid object are properly set up, you must configure the fluid settings to achieve the desired effect. Within the Physics Properties tab, select the type of fluid simulation you need, such as "Liquid" or "Gas." For liquids, you'll find options to adjust viscosity, surface tension, and other properties that influence how the fluid behaves. Viscosity determines how thick or thin the liquid is, affecting its flow and interaction with surfaces. Surface tension affects the cohesion of the liquid, influencing how droplets form and merge.

Additionally, you'll need to set up the inflow and outflow boundaries. Inflow objects are those from which the fluid will enter the domain, while outflow objects allow the fluid to exit. For instance, if you're simulating a pouring cup, the cup itself would be an inflow object, and the domain might include an outflow area to remove excess liquid. After setting up these elements, bake the simulation to generate the fluid's movement. Baking is a crucial step as it processes the simulation data and stores it for playback, ensuring that the fluid behaves consistently during rendering.

For complex simulations involving cloth, Blender offers a powerful set of tools to create and manage fabric interactions. Cloth simulations can replicate the movement of textiles, such as flags fluttering in the wind or clothing draping over a character. To initiate a cloth simulation, select the mesh object that you want to behave like cloth and navigate to the Physics Properties tab. Enable the Cloth option to apply the cloth simulation to the mesh.

Similar to fluid simulations, you'll need to adjust various settings to tailor the cloth behavior to your needs. Key parameters include mass, which affects the weight and drape of the cloth, and stiffness, which determines how rigid or flexible the fabric appears. Additionally, the "Structural" and "Shear" settings control how the cloth resists stretching and tearing. For realistic interactions with other objects, you can define collision settings, ensuring that the cloth properly responds to collisions with other surfaces or characters in the scene.

Once the cloth simulation parameters are set, it's essential to bake the simulation. Baking processes the cloth interactions and calculates the movement of the fabric over time. This step is necessary for accurate playback and rendering of the cloth's behavior. During the baking process, you might need to fine-tune the simulation settings to address any issues, such as cloth penetration or unrealistic stretching.

Blender's physics and simulation tools also include particle systems, which can simulate a variety of effects such as dust, fire, and smoke. Particle systems are highly versatile and can be customized to produce numerous effects based on their settings. For instance, when simulating smoke, you'll configure particle emitters and adjust parameters such as density, temperature, and smoke color. The simulation will then create a particle system that generates and manages the smoke particles, providing a realistic effect that can be used in various scenarios.

Moreover, the integration of these simulations with your animation pipeline requires a careful balance of performance and quality. High-resolution simulations may produce more realistic results but can be computationally expensive and time-consuming to render. Therefore, it is often beneficial to start with lower resolution settings and gradually increase the resolution as needed, ensuring that the final result meets your quality standards while managing rendering times effectively.

Finally, to achieve cohesive results across different types of simulations, consider how they interact with each other within your scene. For example, a fluid simulation interacting with a cloth simulation can create complex effects, such as a liquid soaking into fabric. Ensuring that all simulations are properly configured and baked will contribute to a more seamless and realistic final output. By mastering these advanced simulation techniques and incorporating them effectively into your animations, you will greatly enhance the realism and dynamism of your projects, providing a more engaging experience for your audience.

When refining and managing complex simulations in Blender, you must also pay attention to how simulations interact with one another and with the overall scene. This involves understanding how to balance and optimize your simulations for both performance and visual fidelity.

To start, integrating multiple simulations requires careful planning to ensure that the interactions between different elements are realistic. For instance, if you are combining fluid and cloth simulations, you need to ensure that the fluid interacts correctly with the cloth, such as liquid soaking into or dripping onto the cloth. This requires precise timing and setup, as the fluid simulation must be completed and baked before the cloth simulation begins. You may need to adjust the timing of the simulations so that the fluid has the desired effect on the cloth when rendered.

Blender's cache system is instrumental in managing complex simulations. The cache stores the simulation data after baking, allowing you to preview and render the simulation without recalculating it each time. This feature is crucial for efficiency, especially in projects with multiple or complex simulations. To clear or manage the cache, navigate to the Cache section in the Physics Properties tab. You can delete the cache to free up memory or update it if changes have been made to the simulation settings.

Another important aspect is to use Blender's debugging tools to identify and correct issues in simulations. For instance, if a cloth simulation is not behaving as expected, such as clipping through other objects or not interacting correctly with the wind, you can use the wireframe view and simulation debug options to troubleshoot. The debug view allows you to visualize the underlying mesh and its deformation during the simulation, helping you identify areas that may require adjustments.

In addition to simulation settings, it is essential to consider the hardware limitations and performance optimization. Simulations can be computationally intensive, and managing their impact on your system's performance is vital. To mitigate performance issues, you can use lower-resolution domains and objects for preliminary simulations and increase their resolution for the final render. This approach allows you to test and refine the simulation without taxing your system's resources excessively.

For highly detailed simulations, Blender offers various tools for fine-tuning. The Graph Editor is particularly useful for refining animation curves and simulation data. By accessing the Graph Editor, you can adjust the curves that represent the motion of objects and forces in your simulations, enabling precise control over their behavior. This tool helps smooth out any inconsistencies or abrupt changes in the simulation, contributing to a more polished final output.

Blender's Particle System is another powerful tool that can be integrated with physics simulations. Particles can simulate a wide range of effects, such as dust, sparks, or snow, and can be influenced by other simulations like fluid or cloth. Setting up particle systems involves configuring emitter settings, particle behaviors, and interactions with other objects. The Particle System settings allow you to control aspects such as particle size, lifetime, and emission rate, which are critical for achieving the desired visual effect.

When working with particles in conjunction with other simulations, it is crucial to manage how particles interact with fluids and cloth. For example, particles can be emitted from a fluid surface to simulate splashes or bubbles, or they can be affected by cloth movement to mimic debris or particles falling through fabric. Properly setting up these interactions requires a good understanding of how particles and other simulations influence each other and can involve iterative testing to achieve the desired result.

Finally, always keep in mind the rendering settings related to simulations. For instance, fluid and cloth simulations may require additional memory and processing power during rendering. Optimizing render settings, such as using lower sample rates or simplifying the simulation details for previews, can help manage rendering times and system performance. Once satisfied with the simulations, you can increase the quality settings for the final render to ensure high visual fidelity.

Mastering physics and simulations in Blender enhances your ability to create realistic and dynamic animations. By effectively utilizing Blender's simulation tools, managing their interactions, and optimizing performance, you can bring a high level of realism to your animations, making them engaging and visually compelling. This understanding not only expands your technical skills but also enhances your creative potential, enabling you to tackle more complex and realistic animation projects.

CHAPTER 17: CAMERA ANIMATION AND CINEMATICS

Animating cameras is an essential aspect of creating engaging and dynamic visual narratives. It allows you to guide the viewer's attention, create emotional impact, and enhance the storytelling of your projects. In Blender, the process of animating cameras involves more than just moving them through scenes; it requires a thoughtful approach to camera placement, movement, and integration with other animations to achieve a polished and professional result.

To start with camera animation, you need to understand the fundamental movements that can be applied to the camera. These include pans, tilts, dolly shots, and zooms. Each movement serves a different purpose in storytelling and must be used judiciously to support the narrative. A pan involves rotating the camera horizontally around a fixed point, which is useful for following a character or revealing more of the scene. A tilt, on the other hand, involves rotating the camera vertically, which can be used to emphasize height or depth.

A dolly shot is achieved by physically moving the camera towards or away from the subject, which creates a sense of motion within the scene. This is particularly effective for drawing the viewer's attention to specific elements or characters. Zooming, which changes the camera's focal length, can also be used to adjust the viewer's perspective, though it should be used carefully as it can sometimes create a less natural effect compared to physical movement.

When animating these movements, it is important to create smooth transitions to maintain a cinematic quality. Blender provides several tools to help achieve this, including the Graph Editor and the Dope Sheet. The Graph Editor allows you to adjust the animation curves of your camera's movement, ensuring smooth acceleration and deceleration. This is essential for avoiding abrupt starts or stops, which can be jarring to the viewer. You can fine-tune the speed and smoothness of camera transitions by manipulating these curves to create more natural motion.

The Dope Sheet offers a different perspective by providing a timeline view of your camera's keyframes. This tool is useful for managing and adjusting keyframe placements, ensuring that the timing of camera movements aligns with other elements in your scene. By using both the Graph Editor and the Dope Sheet together, you can achieve a high level of control over your camera animations.

In addition to basic movements, integrating camera animations with character and object animations is crucial for creating a cohesive and immersive experience. This involves coordinating the timing and interaction of all animations within a scene. For example, if a character is performing a significant action, such as a dramatic gesture or a crucial moment, the camera should be positioned and animated to highlight and enhance that action. This requires careful planning and synchronization of the camera's movements with the character's actions.

Blender's constraints and parenting systems can assist with this integration. By parenting the camera to an object or character, you can create animations where the camera follows or interacts with the subject automatically. For example, if you want the camera to follow a character through a scene, you can parent the camera to the character and adjust the relative position to achieve the desired effect. Constraints can also be used to create more complex interactions, such as keeping the camera focused on a specific object while moving through the scene.

When planning camera movements, it is also beneficial to consider the composition and framing of your shots. The rule of thirds is a fundamental principle in cinematography that helps to create balanced and visually appealing compositions. By positioning important elements along the grid lines or at the intersections of these lines, you can guide the viewer's eye and enhance the visual interest of your shots. Blender's camera settings allow you to adjust focal length and depth of field, which further supports effective composition by controlling the area of focus and the overall look of your scene.

Moreover, utilizing depth of field in your camera settings can add a layer of realism and focus to your animations. By adjusting the aperture and focal distance, you can control the amount of blur in the background or foreground, directing the viewer's attention to specific areas of the scene. This technique is particularly useful in creating a sense of depth and highlighting key elements within your animation.

As you advance in camera animation, experimenting with more complex techniques such as camera rigs and virtual cameras can offer additional creative possibilities. Camera rigs allow you to create intricate camera paths and movements that would be difficult to achieve with a single camera alone. Virtual cameras, on the other hand, enable you to set up multiple camera angles and perspectives within a single scene, providing more flexibility in capturing different aspects of your animation.

In summary, animating cameras in Blender involves mastering a variety of movements and techniques to enhance the storytelling and visual impact of your projects. By carefully planning and executing camera animations, integrating them with other animations, and utilizing Blender's tools and settings, you can create compelling and cinematic visuals that captivate and engage your audience.

To create compelling and visually engaging narratives, integrating camera animations with character and object animations is crucial. This integration ensures that camera movements not only follow the action but also enhance the storytelling by highlighting key moments and emotions. A well-executed camera animation can elevate the overall impact of your scene, making it feel more dynamic and immersive.

Start by considering the relationship between your camera and the subjects within your scene. For example, if a character is delivering an important line or making a significant gesture, you might want to animate the camera to focus on this moment. This can be achieved through techniques such as tracking shots, where the camera follows the character's movement, or by using close-ups to emphasize expressions and actions.

When animating the camera to follow a character, you'll typically use keyframes to set the position and orientation of the camera at different points in time. It's important to plan these keyframes carefully to ensure that the camera movement feels natural and complements the character's actions. For instance, if a character is running, a camera that tracks their movement smoothly can create a sense of speed and urgency. Adjusting the camera's path using the Graph Editor will help refine the movement, ensuring that it accelerates and decelerates in a way that feels realistic.

Incorporating object animations into your camera movements can also enhance the narrative. For instance, if a character interacts with an object, such as picking up a book or opening a door, the camera can be animated to focus on these actions, adding detail and context to the scene. This approach requires precise coordination between the camera's path and the object's animation to ensure that the focus remains on the important elements of the scene. Use the Dope Sheet to manage and synchronize keyframes for both the camera and the objects, ensuring that they move in harmony.

Camera movements can also be used to create visual interest and guide the viewer's attention. For example, a slow dolly in can build suspense by gradually revealing a crucial element of the scene, while a quick pan can convey excitement or urgency. The timing of these movements should be carefully planned to align with the pacing of the scene. Use the Timeline to adjust the timing of your camera movements, ensuring that they complement the actions and emotions of the characters.

Moreover, integrating camera animations with lighting changes can further enhance the cinematic quality of your scenes. For example, as the camera moves through a scene, changes in lighting can be used to highlight different aspects or create mood shifts. This requires coordinating the camera animation with light sources to ensure that the lighting enhances the visual narrative. Utilize Blender's lighting tools to adjust the intensity, color, and position of lights as the camera moves, creating a more dynamic and engaging visual experience.

To achieve smooth and professional camera animations, consider employing techniques such as easing and damping. Easing refers to gradually accelerating or decelerating the camera's movement, which helps avoid sudden jerks or abrupt changes in speed. Damping, on the other hand, involves reducing the camera's velocity over time to create a more natural and fluid motion. These techniques can be applied using the Graph Editor, where you can adjust the interpolation of keyframes to control the camera's movement more precisely.

In summary, animating cameras in Blender requires a thoughtful approach to movement, timing, and integration with other animations. By carefully planning and executing camera movements, you can enhance storytelling and create visually compelling scenes that captivate your audience. Mastering these techniques will enable you to add cinematic flair to your projects, making them more dynamic and engaging. Whether you're focusing on character interactions, object animations, or lighting changes, a well-animated camera can significantly elevate the quality and impact of your animations.

To refine camera animations further and integrate them seamlessly into your scene, consider the role of camera transitions and their impact on the narrative flow. Smooth transitions between different camera angles or shots can significantly enhance the storytelling by maintaining the viewer's engagement and guiding their attention.

Start by planning your camera transitions in relation to the narrative structure. For instance, when moving from a wide shot to a close-up, ensure the transition supports the storytelling by highlighting a key detail or emotion. The timing and ease of the transition are critical here; abrupt or poorly timed changes can disrupt the viewer's immersion. Utilize Blender's tools to adjust the interpolation of your camera keyframes to create smooth and natural transitions. The Graph Editor is invaluable in this process, allowing you to fine-tune the motion curves to ensure that the camera accelerates and decelerates smoothly between keyframes.

One technique to achieve seamless transitions is to use camera cuts sparingly and purposefully. For instance, a well-executed cut can shift the viewer's focus effectively from one subject to another, enhancing dramatic impact or providing necessary context. To ensure that cuts do not feel jarring, align them with significant narrative beats or changes in the scene. The timing of these cuts should match the rhythm of the animation and the pacing of the action.

In addition to handling camera transitions, integrating camera movements with character animations requires careful coordination. For instance, if a character is walking across the scene, the camera might follow their path with a tracking shot. Adjust the camera's path to match the character's movement, ensuring that it maintains the intended focus and framing. Use the Timeline and Dope Sheet to synchronize the character's and camera's keyframes, ensuring that the camera's movement complements the character's actions without overshadowing them.

Another aspect to consider is the depth of field and focus in your camera animations. By adjusting the focal length and aperture settings, you can create a shallow depth of field that directs attention to specific elements within the frame, such as a character's face or a crucial object. This technique enhances the cinematic quality of your animations and helps to emphasize important details. Blender's camera settings provide options for controlling depth of field, allowing you to create a more polished and professional look.

When dealing with complex scenes involving multiple cameras or dynamic changes in perspective, it's essential to manage camera layers and sequences effectively. Blender's Multi-Cam feature allows you to set up and switch between multiple camera views within a single scene. This capability is particularly useful for scenes requiring different perspectives or angles, such as a dialogue scene with alternating close-ups and wide shots. Use the Sequence Editor to manage and arrange these camera angles, ensuring that transitions between different perspectives are smooth and coherent.

In addition to camera settings, consider the impact of camera movements on the overall composition and visual storytelling. For example, using a low-angle shot can create a sense of power or dominance for a character, while a high-angle shot can make them appear vulnerable or diminished. The framing and composition of your shots should support the narrative and character development, adding depth to the visual storytelling.

Lastly, don't overlook the importance of reviewing and iterating on your camera animations. After setting up your camera movements and transitions, review the animation in the context of the entire scene. Pay attention to how the camera's movements interact with the character and object animations, and adjust as needed to ensure that the final result is cohesive and visually compelling. Gathering feedback from others can also provide valuable insights and help identify areas for improvement.

By mastering these techniques and incorporating them into your workflow, you can enhance your animations with dynamic and engaging camera work that supports and enriches the storytelling. Camera animation is a powerful tool in creating immersive and visually captivating projects, and with practice and attention to detail, you'll be able to bring your scenes to life with greater control and precision.

CHAPTER 18: LIGHTING AND RENDERING TECHNIQUES

Advanced lighting and rendering techniques are crucial for achieving professional-quality visuals in your projects. With a firm grasp on the fundamentals, it's time to explore how to elevate your work using more sophisticated methods, focusing on global illumination, detailed render settings, and advanced shading techniques.

Start by understanding global illumination (GI), which simulates the complex interactions of light within a scene to produce more realistic results. GI is essential for creating natural-looking environments where light bounces off surfaces and contributes to the overall illumination. Blender offers several approaches to global illumination, including indirect lighting and photon mapping. To effectively use GI, you need to adjust the settings of your render engine, which may involve enabling global illumination features and configuring parameters like bounce settings, intensity, and distance.

In Blender, using the Cycles rendering engine provides a robust platform for working with global illumination. For instance, Cycles uses path tracing to calculate how light travels through a scene, which can be particularly useful for achieving high levels of realism. To harness Cycles' global illumination capabilities, you should enable features like "Bounces" in the Render Settings tab. This allows you to control the number of light bounces that occur, influencing the quality and realism of your render. It's often beneficial to start with a higher number of bounces for detailed scenes and reduce it for faster preview renders.

When it comes to render settings, optimizing them for different outputs is key to balancing quality and performance. Blender's render settings offer a range of parameters to adjust, including resolution, sampling rates, and denoising options. Higher resolution settings will produce more detailed images, but at the cost of increased render times. Sampling rates, both for the render and viewport, influence the level of detail and noise in the final output. Increasing the number of samples generally improves quality but requires longer render times. For efficient workflow, it's advisable to use lower samples for test renders and higher samples for final outputs.

Denoising is another crucial aspect of rendering. Blender provides several denoising options to reduce noise in your renders, such as the built-in denoiser available in the Cycles engine. This feature smooths out noise that can result from low sampling rates, enhancing the overall quality of your image. The denoising settings can be adjusted to balance between preserving detail and removing noise effectively.

Advanced shading techniques further enhance the realism and visual appeal of your renders. Shaders define how surfaces interact with light and include options such as diffuse, specular, and emissive materials. To achieve more complex materials, you can use Blender's node-based shader editor, which allows for detailed control over how shaders are combined and manipulated. For example, combining diffuse and glossy shaders can create realistic surfaces like polished wood or metal. Utilizing nodes such as the Principled BSDF shader provides a versatile and powerful way to create a wide range of materials with accurate physical properties.

Another important shading technique is the use of texture mapping, which involves applying 2D images or patterns onto 3D models to add detail and variation. Textures can influence various aspects of a material, including color, bumpiness, and reflectivity. In Blender, texture maps such as diffuse, bump, and normal maps can be used to achieve different effects. For instance, a bump map adds surface detail without altering the geometry, while a normal map provides more intricate surface details that respond to light.

Lighting setup is a critical component of rendering and can dramatically impact the final look of your scene. Blender offers various light types, including point lights, sun lamps, spotlights, and area lights. Each type serves different purposes and can be combined to create the desired illumination effects. For realistic lighting, it's essential to consider the interplay of different light sources, their intensities, and their positions relative to objects in the scene. Additionally, using HDRI (High Dynamic Range Imaging) environment maps can provide realistic ambient lighting and reflections, enhancing the overall realism of the render.

Blender's render engines, such as Eevee and Cycles, offer different approaches to achieving high-quality results. Eevee is a real-time renderer that provides fast preview and final renders, making it suitable for projects requiring quick turnaround times. On the other hand, Cycles is a path-tracing renderer that excels in producing high-quality, photorealistic images but requires more computational power and time.

By mastering these advanced lighting and rendering techniques, you can achieve more polished and professional results in your animations and visual projects. Understanding how to leverage global illumination, optimize render settings, and employ sophisticated shading methods will significantly enhance the visual quality of your work, allowing you to create stunning and impactful images.

To further refine your lighting and rendering skills, it's crucial to explore advanced shading techniques that contribute to the realism and impact of your visual projects. Shading is the process of defining how surfaces interact with light, and mastering it can dramatically enhance the quality of your renders.

In Blender, shaders are primarily managed through the Shader Editor, where you can create and modify materials using a node-based system. The core shaders in Blender include Diffuse BSDF, Glossy BSDF, and Principled BSDF, each of which has its own role in how light interacts with surfaces. The Principled BSDF shader is particularly versatile, offering a wide range of controls for creating realistic materials. It combines several shading models into one, allowing you to adjust properties such as base color, roughness, metallicity, and specular reflections. For most materials, the Principled BSDF shader provides a comprehensive solution, but for specialized needs, you might still use individual shaders like Glossy or Emission.

When working with shaders, it's essential to understand how different materials react to light. For example, a Glossy shader simulates reflective surfaces and is ideal for creating materials like metals or glass. Adjusting parameters such as roughness can control the sharpness of reflections, while the IOR (Index of Refraction) setting helps achieve accurate glass and water effects. On the other hand, the Diffuse shader is suited for matte surfaces, where light is scattered rather than reflected.

Textures play a significant role in shading, providing detailed surface information that influences how materials look under various lighting conditions. In Blender, textures are applied through nodes in the Shader Editor, where you can link them to different properties of your shaders. Texture maps, such as diffuse maps, bump maps, and normal maps, allow you to add complexity to your materials. A diffuse map determines the base color of a surface, while bump and normal maps simulate small surface imperfections and details that affect how light interacts with the surface.

Bump maps create the illusion of surface texture by modifying the surface normal, affecting how light is reflected without altering the actual geometry. Normal maps offer a more detailed and realistic simulation of surface features by encoding more complex surface information, providing finer detail than bump maps. These textures enhance the visual complexity of materials without increasing polygon count, which is crucial for optimizing render times and maintaining performance.

In addition to these techniques, it's essential to consider lighting setups and their impact on shading. The placement and type of lights in a scene will influence how materials appear. For instance, using HDRIs (High Dynamic Range Images) for environment lighting can provide realistic lighting and reflections by simulating a real-world light source. HDRIs capture a wide range of light intensities and colors, contributing to more accurate and immersive lighting effects. They are particularly effective for scenes where natural or complex lighting conditions are required.

Advanced shading also involves understanding and using shaders for specific effects. For example, subsurface scattering (SSS) shaders are used for materials like skin, wax, or marble, where light penetrates the surface and scatters internally before being reflected. The SSS shader allows for the simulation of this light behavior, providing a softer and more realistic appearance for materials that are not perfectly opaque.

To achieve high-quality renders, combining these advanced shading techniques with effective lighting setups and optimized render settings is crucial. Each element—shaders, textures, and lights—works together to create a cohesive and visually appealing final image. Testing and adjusting these elements iteratively will help you achieve the desired look and ensure that your animations or stills are both striking and realistic.

By integrating global illumination, optimizing render settings, and employing advanced shading techniques, you will enhance your ability to create professional-quality visuals. Understanding these concepts in depth will not only improve the realism of your scenes but also allow you to push the boundaries of what is possible in your 3D projects.

In addition to the foundational shaders and textures, mastering global illumination (GI) is essential for creating realistic lighting effects. Global illumination encompasses the various ways light is bounced around a scene, including the indirect lighting that occurs when light reflects off surfaces and illuminates other areas. This technique adds depth and realism by simulating how light interacts with the environment beyond direct light sources.

Blender offers two primary methods for achieving global illumination: ray tracing and screen space reflections. Ray tracing, employed by the Cycles rendering engine, calculates the paths of light rays as they bounce through a scene, providing accurate results but requiring more computational power. Cycles' ability to handle complex light interactions, such as caustics and multiple bounces, makes it ideal for high-quality renders where precision is crucial.

For faster but less accurate global illumination, Blender's Eevee rendering engine uses screen space reflections and approximations. Eevee is designed for real-time rendering and can simulate GI through methods like approximate reflections and ambient occlusion. Although it does not offer the same level of detail as Cycles, Eevee's speed makes it suitable for previewing animations or projects where rendering time is a concern.

To effectively utilize global illumination in Blender, you need to adjust several settings in the Render Properties tab. For Cycles, enable "Global Illumination" and adjust parameters such as the number of bounces and the sampling rate to control the quality and performance of your render. Higher bounce settings will improve the realism of light interactions but may increase render times. In Eevee, enable options like "Screen Space Reflections" and "Ambient Occlusion" to approximate global illumination effects, and fine-tune these settings to balance visual fidelity with performance.

Another critical aspect of advanced rendering is optimizing render settings for different outputs. This involves adjusting parameters to suit the resolution, quality, and file format required for your final render. Higher resolutions and quality settings enhance detail and clarity but significantly increase render times and resource usage. To manage these trade-offs, you should understand the implications of settings such as resolution, sampling, and output format.

Resolution determines the size of the final image or animation, with higher resolutions offering greater detail. However, increasing resolution also demands more processing power and memory. For animation, consider rendering at a lower resolution for previews and then performing a final high-resolution render for the final output. Sampling controls the number of rays traced per pixel and affects the clarity and noise levels in your render. Higher sampling rates improve image quality but extend render times, so finding a balance is crucial.

Output format plays a significant role in how your rendered images or animations are saved and compressed. Blender supports various formats, including JPEG, PNG, and TIFF for still images, and formats like MP4 or AVI for animations. For lossless quality, formats such as PNG or TIFF are preferable, though they result in larger file sizes. For compressed outputs, JPEG or video formats like H.264 offer smaller file sizes at the expense of some quality loss.

Finally, creating stunning visual effects often involves using Blender's compositing tools, which allow you to enhance and refine your rendered images or animations. Compositing involves combining multiple render passes and applying various effects to achieve the desired look. For example, you can use passes like diffuse, specular, and shadow passes to fine-tune the final appearance of your render. Blender's Compositor provides a node-based interface where you can blend, adjust, and enhance different elements of your render, applying effects such as color correction, depth of field, and motion blur.

By combining these advanced techniques—global illumination, optimized render settings, and compositing—you can achieve professional-quality results that enhance the realism and impact of your visual projects. Mastery of these elements will enable you to create more dynamic and visually compelling animations, elevating your work to new levels of sophistication and polish.

CHAPTER 19: POST-PROCESSING AND COMPOSITING

To achieve a polished and professional finish in your animations, post-processing and compositing are critical stages in the production pipeline. In Blender, these processes are facilitated through a powerful suite of tools that allow you to refine, enhance, and perfect your renders. By integrating various effects, color corrections, and compositional techniques, you can elevate the visual quality of your projects and ensure that the final output meets your creative vision.

The heart of Blender's compositing capabilities lies in the node-based system. Nodes provide a flexible and modular approach to compositing, enabling you to apply a series of effects and adjustments in a non-linear fashion. This method not only enhances the efficiency of your workflow but also offers greater control over the final appearance of your animations.

Begin by accessing Blender's Compositing workspace, which provides a node editor specifically designed for compositing tasks. Here, you can create and connect nodes to build your compositing network. The basic nodes include input nodes for your rendered images, output nodes for exporting the final product, and a variety of filter nodes for applying effects. Each node performs a specific function, such as color correction, blurring, or adding visual effects, and can be adjusted through its properties to fine-tune the result.

A fundamental component of compositing is color grading, which involves adjusting the color properties of your renders to achieve the desired mood or aesthetic. Blender offers several color correction nodes, such as the Color Balance, Hue/Saturation, and RGB Curves nodes. These tools allow you to manipulate color channels, adjust brightness and contrast, and apply color grading presets to achieve a specific look. For instance, you might use the RGB Curves node to enhance the contrast in a scene or the Hue/Saturation node to shift the overall color palette.

Another important aspect of compositing is integrating additional visual effects. Blender's node system includes a range of effect nodes, such as Blur, Glare, and Glow, which can be used to enhance the visual impact of your animation. The Glare node, for example, can simulate lens flares or light blooms, adding a cinematic quality to your renders. The Blur node helps in softening edges or creating depth-of-field effects, which can be particularly useful in achieving a more realistic look.

To achieve seamless integration of these effects, you must carefully manage the compositing layers and their interactions. Blender allows you to layer multiple effects and corrections, each affecting the final output in distinct ways. For example, you might apply a color correction layer followed by a blur effect to create a desired look. Managing the order and intensity of these layers is crucial to avoid artifacts and ensure a cohesive final product.

Once your compositing network is set up, you can preview the results directly within Blender. Use the Viewer node to view your composited output in real-time, allowing you to make iterative adjustments and see the effects of changes immediately. This real-time feedback is invaluable for fine-tuning the appearance of your animation and ensuring that all elements are well integrated.

For exporting the final composited animation, configure the Output Properties settings to select the desired file format and resolution. Blender supports various formats, including PNG, JPEG, and video formats like MP4. Choose the format that best suits your needs and adjust the settings for compression and quality as necessary. It's often beneficial to render out a high-quality version of the final animation to preserve detail and clarity.

Additionally, Blender's Render Layers feature allows you to render different elements of your scene separately and composite them together in post-processing. This technique is useful for managing complex scenes with multiple objects and effects. By rendering layers such as foreground, background, and special effects separately, you can have greater control over each element in the compositing stage.

The final step in post-processing is to review the animation thoroughly, ensuring that all visual effects are cohesive and that color grading enhances the overall aesthetic. Pay close attention to transitions between scenes, any potential artifacts introduced during compositing, and the overall visual impact of the animation. This comprehensive review process is essential for delivering a high-quality, professional result.

Mastering the art of post-processing and compositing in Blender empowers you to enhance your animations significantly, creating visually compelling and polished final products. By leveraging the node-based system, color grading tools, and effect nodes, you can refine your animations to meet the highest standards of visual excellence.

To achieve seamless integration of visual effects and ensure a cohesive final product, you must consider several advanced compositing techniques. These techniques enable you to refine your animations by combining rendered layers, applying nuanced effects, and addressing any discrepancies that may arise during the rendering process.

One essential technique in compositing is working with render layers. Render layers allow you to separate different elements of your scene into distinct layers, such as foreground, background, and effects. By compositing these layers individually, you can manage and tweak each element separately, which provides greater flexibility and control over the final look of your animation. To utilize render layers effectively, you start by setting up your scene to render multiple passes, such as diffuse, specular, and shadow passes. Each pass captures specific aspects of your scene, which can then be combined in the compositor to achieve the desired result. For example, you might use a shadow pass to fine-tune the shadows independently of the rest of the scene, ensuring they blend seamlessly with the background.

The use of masks and alpha channels is another vital technique in compositing. Masks allow you to define specific areas of an image that will be affected by certain effects or adjustments. By creating masks, you can isolate and apply changes to particular regions of your rendered image without affecting the entire frame. For instance, if you need to adjust the brightness of just one part of your animation, you can use a mask to limit the adjustment to that area. Alpha channels, on the other hand, handle transparency information in your images. When compositing layers, you can use alpha channels to control how layers blend together, ensuring that transparent areas are handled correctly and that the final composition appears natural and integrated.

Depth of field effects can significantly enhance the realism of your animations. By simulating the way real cameras focus on objects at different distances, you can add a layer of sophistication to your visuals. In Blender's compositor, you can apply depth of field effects by utilizing the Z-Depth pass, which provides information about the distance of objects from the camera. This pass can be combined with a defocus node to blur parts of the image based on their distance from the camera, creating a realistic depth-of-field effect. Adjusting the parameters of the defocus node allows you to control the amount of blur and the focus range, tailoring the effect to suit your project's needs.

Color correction is another crucial aspect of compositing, as it ensures that the colors in your animation are consistent and visually appealing. Beyond basic color grading, advanced color correction techniques involve using curves and masks to make specific adjustments. For example, you might use the Curves node to adjust the color balance across different color channels, fine-tuning the hues to achieve a specific look. Additionally, combining color correction with masks allows you to make targeted adjustments, such as enhancing the color of a character while keeping the background colors unchanged.

When integrating visual effects, consider the interaction between various elements in your scene. For instance, adding visual effects like smoke, fire, or particles requires careful compositing to ensure that these effects blend naturally with the rest of the animation. This often involves adjusting the transparency, blending modes, and color balance of the effect layers to achieve a convincing integration. Using the Alpha Over node, you can layer effects on top of your primary renders, adjusting their opacity and blending them with the underlying layers to achieve a seamless result.

Finally, optimizing your compositing workflow is essential for managing complex projects efficiently. Blender provides several tools and features to streamline the compositing process, including the ability to create custom node groups and utilize templates. Custom node groups allow you to bundle a set of nodes into a single, reusable node, simplifying your node setup and reducing clutter in the node editor. Templates, on the other hand, enable you to save and reuse compositing setups across multiple projects, ensuring consistency and saving time.

By mastering these advanced compositing techniques, you can enhance the quality and visual impact of your animations, creating a polished and professional final product. Understanding and applying these methods will not only improve the aesthetic appeal of your work but also provide you with the tools to tackle complex compositing challenges with confidence.

Once you have mastered the fundamentals of compositing and post-processing, you can delve into more advanced techniques to further elevate the quality of your animations. One such technique is the use of color grading, which involves adjusting the colors and tones of your rendered images to achieve a specific mood or visual style. Blender's compositor provides a variety of tools for color grading, such as the Color Balance node, which allows you to adjust the shadows, midtones, and highlights separately. This node enables precise control over the color palette of your animation, helping you to create a cohesive and visually striking look.

Additionally, the use of the RGB Curves node is another powerful method for fine-tuning color and contrast. The RGB Curves node lets you manipulate the individual color channels (red, green, and blue) as well as the overall luminance of your image. By adjusting the curves, you can enhance contrast, correct color imbalances, and refine the overall tone of your animation. This technique is especially useful for achieving high dynamic range (HDR) effects or correcting color inconsistencies that may arise during the rendering process.

Incorporating visual effects such as lens flares, glows, and particle effects can also add a professional touch to your animations. Blender's compositor offers nodes such as the Glare node, which simulates the effects of lens flares and glowing highlights. The Glare node provides options for various types of glare effects, including streaks, ghosts, and fog, which can be adjusted to match the visual style of your project. Similarly, particle effects can be composited using the Render Layers and Particle nodes, allowing you to integrate effects like smoke, fire, or rain into your animation seamlessly.

Another crucial aspect of post-processing is optimizing the final output for different formats and resolutions. Blender's render settings allow you to choose from various output formats, such as JPEG, PNG, and EXR, each with its own set of advantages. For high-quality results, especially in professional production environments, EXR is often preferred due to its support for high dynamic range and lossless compression. Additionally, you may need to adjust the resolution and aspect ratio of your animation to fit specific display requirements or deliverables. Blender provides options for scaling and cropping the output, ensuring that your animation appears correctly on different screens and platforms.

As you finalize your animation, it is also important to consider the rendering and compositing performance. Large, complex scenes with high-resolution textures and multiple effects can lead to long render times and potential performance issues. To address this, you can employ various optimization techniques, such as simplifying geometry, reducing texture sizes, and using render passes to isolate and render specific elements separately. By optimizing your scene and render settings, you can achieve a balance between visual quality and performance, ensuring efficient rendering without compromising the final output.

Throughout the post-processing and compositing phase, it is essential to continually review and critique your work. Regularly previewing your animation with different settings and adjustments will help you identify areas for improvement and ensure that the final product meets your artistic vision. Utilizing tools such as Blender's viewer node and render previews can provide valuable feedback and guide you in making the necessary refinements.

In conclusion, mastering post-processing and compositing techniques in Blender requires a combination of technical knowledge and artistic sensibility. By leveraging advanced tools and methods, you can enhance your animations, correct color imbalances, and integrate sophisticated visual effects, ultimately achieving a polished and professional result. The skills and techniques discussed here will empower you to create captivating and high-quality animations, elevating your projects to a level of excellence that reflects both your creativity and technical expertise.

CHAPTER 20: CHARACTER ANIMATION AND EXPRESSIONS

Character animation extends beyond the mere articulation of movements; it involves breathing life into characters through detailed expressions and emotional depth. Achieving this requires a nuanced approach to animating facial expressions and gestures, pivotal in conveying the full spectrum of human emotions. In this segment, we will delve into the sophisticated techniques required for creating compelling and believable character animations, focusing on shape keys and drivers to manipulate facial features and gestures effectively.

To begin with, understanding the role of shape keys in character animation is essential. Shape keys, also known as blend shapes, allow you to morph a character's mesh into various predefined shapes. These shapes can represent different facial expressions, such as smiles, frowns, or surprise. By creating a series of shape keys for these expressions, you can blend between them to achieve a wide range of emotions.

Start by selecting your character model and entering the Object Data Properties panel. Here, you can find the Shape Keys section where you will create and manage your shape keys. Begin with the base shape key, which represents the neutral expression of your character. From this base, add new shape keys for each desired expression. For instance, if you want to create a surprised look, adjust the mesh to reflect raised eyebrows, wide eyes, and a slightly open mouth. Once satisfied, click on the "+" button to create a new shape key with this expression. Repeat this process for other emotions like happiness, anger, or sadness.

After setting up your shape keys, you need to control how these expressions blend together. This is where drivers come into play. Drivers are variables that influence the value of shape keys based on different inputs, such as sliders or other properties. For example, you can use drivers to control the intensity of a smile based on the character's mood or the context of the scene.

To set up a driver, first, select the shape key you want to control and right-click on the value slider in the Shape Keys panel. Choose "Add Driver" from the context menu. This action opens the Graph Editor, where you can configure the driver. In the Graph Editor, you will set up the driver to respond to specific inputs. For instance, you might link the smile shape key to a custom property or a control bone in your rig that represents the character's mood.

In addition to shape keys and drivers, animating gestures and body language adds another layer of depth to character animations. Gestures, such as hand movements, body tilts, and posture changes, play a crucial role in conveying emotions and intentions. To animate gestures effectively, focus on the timing and weight of the movements. Use reference materials or motion capture data to guide the animation, ensuring that the gestures match the character's emotional state and narrative context.

Consider the principles of animation, such as squash and stretch, anticipation, and follow-through, when animating gestures. For example, when a character makes a quick gesture, such as a sudden hand movement, the follow-through motion should convey the impact of the movement. Similarly, anticipate the gesture by adding subtle preparatory motions, which enhance the realism and fluidity of the animation.

Facial expressions often work in tandem with body language to create a cohesive portrayal of emotion. Ensure that the facial expressions align with the character's overall body language and actions. For instance, if a character is surprised, their eyes and mouth should reflect this surprise, while their body posture might also exhibit a reaction such as a recoil or a sudden movement.

Finally, refining your character animations involves reviewing and adjusting the animations to ensure consistency and believability. Playback your animations in real-time and analyze the character's expressions and gestures to identify areas for improvement. Make use of animation curves and keyframe adjustments to smooth out transitions and enhance the fluidity of the movements. Pay attention to subtleties, such as eye movements or slight changes in facial expression, as these small details contribute significantly to the overall impact of the animation.

By mastering these techniques, you will be able to create characters that are not only visually appealing but also emotionally engaging. The ability to animate facial expressions and gestures with precision and depth is crucial in bringing characters to life and making them resonate with audiences. As you continue to practice and refine your skills, you'll find that these techniques will become second nature, allowing you to focus on crafting compelling stories and experiences through your animations.

Continuing from the initial exploration of shape keys and drivers, it's crucial to consider the integration of these elements into your overall character rig. This process ensures that expressions are not only varied but also seamlessly incorporated into the character's movement and interactions.

One of the primary considerations is to establish a robust rigging system that includes facial bones or controls. These controls are essential for fine-tuning expressions and achieving a natural blend with the character's body movements. When rigging the face, consider adding control bones or custom properties that can interact with your shape keys. This setup allows you to manipulate expressions in real-time while the character performs various actions. For example, if your character is animated to show surprise, the facial rig should be able to synchronize with the body's movement, such as widening the eyes in response to sudden changes in the scene.

To achieve this, you will need to carefully weight the facial rig. This involves assigning vertex groups to facial bones and ensuring that each shape key affects the mesh appropriately. Rigging tools in Blender, such as the Armature system, can assist with this process. Create bones for key facial features such as the eyebrows, eyelids, and mouth. These bones should be linked to the corresponding shape keys to ensure that as the bones move, the shape keys adjust accordingly. This method facilitates more complex and realistic expressions, as the character's face will react dynamically to various animations.

Another important aspect of character animation is the creation of gesture animations. Gestures, such as hand movements or head tilts, play a significant role in conveying emotion and intent. To animate gestures effectively, you need to understand the principles of motion and how they contribute to the character's emotional state. For example, a character expressing frustration may have clenched fists or a tense posture, while a gesture of joy could include open arms or a relaxed stance.

In Blender, you can animate gestures by setting keyframes for the relevant bones or control points. Begin by defining the key poses for each gesture, ensuring that they align with the character's emotional state. Use interpolation techniques to create smooth transitions between these poses. For instance, if animating a character's hand raising in excitement, start by positioning the hand at the base position, then set additional keyframes at intervals as the hand moves upwards. Adjust the interpolation type in the Graph Editor to achieve the desired fluidity.

Additionally, animating gestures requires attention to timing and spacing. Timing refers to the duration of the gesture and how quickly it occurs, while spacing deals with the distance traveled by the animated parts. Effective timing and spacing will help to convey the appropriate intensity of the gesture. For example, a swift, sharp hand movement might indicate urgency, whereas a slow, deliberate gesture could suggest calmness or contemplation.

Facial animation also benefits greatly from attention to the subtleties of expression. Small changes in the character's face can significantly impact the overall emotion conveyed. Techniques such as blending shape keys for nuanced expressions are invaluable. For example, blending a slight furrow of the brow with a subtle widening of the eyes can convey concern or confusion more effectively than a single, static expression.

Moreover, the combination of facial expressions with body language can enhance the believability of your character. For instance, a character who is angry might not only have a scowling face but also exhibit tense posture and rapid, jerky movements. The integration of these elements requires a comprehensive approach to animation, where each part of the character's body is animated in harmony with the others.

In practice, achieving such synchronization involves continuous review and adjustment of your animations. As you animate, regularly playback your work and observe how well the facial expressions and gestures integrate with the overall performance. Look for any inconsistencies or unnatural movements and make adjustments as needed. This iterative process is crucial for creating polished and believable animations.

Lastly, consider using reference footage to guide your animation. Observing real-life examples of how people express different emotions can provide valuable insights into achieving realistic and engaging animations. By studying these references, you can better understand the nuances of facial expressions and gestures and apply them effectively to your character animations.

In conclusion, animating characters involves a sophisticated interplay of facial expressions, gestures, and body movements. Mastering the use of shape keys, drivers, and a well-rigged character model is essential for creating animations that are not only dynamic but also rich in emotional depth. By integrating these techniques, you can produce animations that resonate with audiences and bring your characters to life with authenticity and engagement.

When refining character animations, especially focusing on expressions and gestures, it's essential to integrate detailed layering and blending techniques. This level of detail ensures that the character's movements are both fluid and natural, enhancing their emotional impact.

Consider the integration of expression layers within the animation timeline. Blender's Nonlinear Animation (NLA) editor allows for the layering of different actions, including facial expressions and gestures. By creating separate actions for various expressions, such as joy, sadness, or anger, and then blending these with the character's main animation sequence, you can achieve nuanced performances. For instance, if a character is laughing while running, the laughter can be animated as a distinct action layer that blends seamlessly with the running motion. Adjusting the influence of these layers in the NLA editor helps you fine-tune the impact of each expression relative to the primary movement.

The Graph Editor is another powerful tool in this process. It enables precise control over animation curves, which is crucial for achieving natural and fluid transitions in facial expressions. In the Graph Editor, you can manipulate the keyframes of shape keys and bone positions to smooth out abrupt changes and ensure that expressions evolve gradually. For example, when animating a character's surprise, ensure that the keyframes for opening the eyes and raising the eyebrows are adjusted to create a smooth, believable reaction. The use of bezier curves in the Graph Editor allows you to manage the acceleration and deceleration of these changes, which is vital for capturing the subtleties of human emotions.

In addition to expressions and gestures, consider how body language complements facial animations. Synchronizing body language with facial expressions enriches the character's overall portrayal. For example, a character who is nervous might fidget with their hands or avoid eye contact, in addition to displaying a worried facial expression. To achieve this, animate both the body and facial expressions in tandem, ensuring that changes in one are reflected in the other. This holistic approach creates a more convincing and engaging character performance.

The use of drivers can further enhance this integration. Drivers in Blender allow you to link the values of one property to another, creating dependencies that can automate and synchronize actions. For example, you might use a driver to link the character's mouth movement with the intensity of a smile, so that as the smile grows wider, the mouth's shape adjusts accordingly. This automated relationship ensures consistency and realism across the animation.

Another consideration is the use of pose libraries. Pose libraries enable you to save and reuse specific facial expressions or gestures. This can be particularly useful for maintaining consistency across multiple scenes or animations. By creating a library of frequently used poses, you can quickly apply and adjust these poses as needed, streamlining the animation process and ensuring that your character's expressions remain coherent.

It's also important to test and review your animations frequently. Playblast previews allow you to quickly review the animation in real-time without rendering. This helps you identify any issues with timing, expression, or synchronization early in the process. Iterative testing and feedback are key to refining animations and achieving the desired emotional impact.

Finally, consider the role of feedback in your animation workflow. Collaborate with others to get fresh perspectives on your work. Sometimes, an external review can provide insights into areas that may need improvement or adjustment, which can be invaluable in achieving a high-quality final product.

By focusing on these advanced techniques and tools, you can create character animations that are rich in emotion and depth. The careful application of shape keys, drivers, and layering, combined with ongoing testing and feedback, will enable you to produce animations that are not only visually compelling but also deeply expressive and engaging.

CHAPTER 21: CREATING AND USING ASSETS

In the realm of large-scale animation and modeling projects, the ability to manage and efficiently reuse assets is crucial for maintaining both productivity and consistency. Understanding how to create, organize, and integrate assets effectively can significantly streamline your workflow, making it easier to handle complex projects and collaborate with other artists.

Creating assets begins with a clear understanding of what you need. Models, textures, and animations are fundamental components, each requiring careful attention to detail. To ensure your assets are reusable and adaptable, consider the following strategies:

Model Creation and Optimization: When creating 3D models, focus on building clean, efficient geometry. This involves minimizing polygon count while retaining necessary detail, a process known as optimization. High-polygon models can be cumbersome, so consider using techniques such as normal maps to add detail without increasing the polygon count. Additionally, ensure that your models are properly UV unwrapped, which means that the 3D surface is flattened into a 2D plane. This step is crucial for applying textures accurately and avoiding texture stretching.

Texture Mapping and Material Setup: Textures play a significant role in giving models their appearance. Create high-quality textures by capturing real-world details or designing them in a graphics editor. Use Blender's UV mapping tools to project textures onto your models, ensuring that the UVs are laid out efficiently to prevent visible seams or distortions. Materials in Blender can be complex, involving shaders and nodes to define how surfaces interact with light. Properly setting up materials with accurate shaders will contribute to realistic rendering outcomes.

Animation Assets: Animations should be crafted with both the character and the scene in mind. For character animations, use rigs that are well-structured and flexible. Create animations that can be reused across different characters by employing a consistent rigging system. Animations can be stored and managed in Blender's Action Editor, where they can be easily accessed and reused for different projects. Consider creating an animation library with commonly used actions like walk cycles or idle poses, which can be applied to various characters with minimal adjustment.

Organizing Asset Libraries: A well-organized asset library is a key to efficient workflow. In Blender, asset libraries can be created by saving models, textures, and animations in a centralized location. Use descriptive naming conventions and categorize assets into folders based on their type or purpose. For instance, you might have separate folders for character models, environment assets, and textures. This organization facilitates quick retrieval and integration of assets into new projects.

Integrating External Resources: Incorporating external resources can greatly enhance your project. Blender supports various file formats, allowing you to import models, textures, and animations created in other software. When integrating external assets, ensure compatibility by checking the import settings and adjusting them as needed. Keep in mind that external resources should be optimized and tested within your

Blender environment to ensure they function correctly and fit within your project's requirements.

Using Asset Packs: Asset packs are collections of pre-made assets that can be a valuable resource for speeding up production. Blender has a range of asset packs available, both free and paid. These packs can include everything from textures and shaders to complete models and animations. When using asset packs, consider customizing the assets to fit the specific needs of your project. This might involve adjusting textures, re-rigging models, or modifying animations to ensure they blend seamlessly with your work.

Version Control and Asset Management: In a collaborative environment or when working on long-term projects, managing different versions of assets is crucial. Implement version control practices to track changes and maintain a history of modifications. This can be achieved through naming conventions that include version numbers or using dedicated version control systems. Effective asset management ensures that updates and revisions are properly documented and that you can revert to previous versions if necessary.

Documentation and Metadata: Providing documentation for your assets enhances their usability and ensures that anyone who uses them can understand their purpose and limitations. Include metadata such as asset descriptions, usage instructions, and any dependencies or constraints. This information is particularly valuable when assets are shared among team members or when they are part of a larger asset library.

By mastering these practices for creating and managing assets, you can improve both the quality and efficiency of your animation and modeling projects. Well-organized and reusable assets not only save time but also ensure consistency and high standards across your work. As you become more adept at handling assets, you'll find that your workflow becomes more streamlined, allowing you to focus on creativity and innovation in your projects.

Managing and reusing assets effectively involves not just their creation but also their organization and integration into various projects. Once you have established a system for creating high-quality models, textures, and animations, the next critical step is to implement a structured approach for organizing and integrating these assets to maximize productivity and consistency across projects.

Building an Asset Library: An organized asset library is a cornerstone of efficient asset management. Begin by structuring your asset library into clear categories based on asset types and their intended use. For instance, separate categories might include environment models, character models, props, textures, and animations. Within these categories, further subdivide assets into specific types or themes, such as urban environments, natural landscapes, or different types of clothing for characters.

When saving assets, use a consistent naming convention that clearly describes the asset's function and characteristics. For example, name a model file "UrbanBuilding_02" rather than something generic like "building". This practice not only helps in quick identification but also prevents confusion when assets are shared among team members.

Using Asset Packs: Asset packs are a valuable resource, especially for quickly prototyping or expanding a project without the need to create every asset from scratch. These packs often include pre-made models, textures, and animations that can be integrated into your project. When working with asset packs, ensure they are compatible with your project's specifications, such as scale, style, and format. It's also crucial to understand the licensing and usage rights associated with these packs to avoid any legal complications.

In Blender, asset packs can be imported directly into your project. Use Blender's Asset Browser to manage and access these assets efficiently. The Asset Browser allows you to preview and drag assets into your scene with ease. For better integration, consider adjusting the assets to match the visual and functional requirements of your project. This may involve tweaking materials, scaling models, or modifying animations to ensure consistency with your project's aesthetic and technical standards.

Integrating External Resources: In addition to creating and managing internal assets, integrating external resources can significantly enhance your projects. External resources include third-party models, textures, plugins, and scripts that can add functionality or improve the quality of your work. When integrating these resources, ensure they are compatible with Blender and your project's requirements.

Blender allows for the integration of various external resources through its import/export functionalities. For instance, you can import textures or models from other software or online resources and apply them to your Blender project. Additionally, scripts and plugins can be added to extend Blender's capabilities, such as enhancing rendering features or adding new animation tools. It is important to keep track of the external resources you integrate, as they may affect the project's performance and compatibility.

Optimizing Asset Management: Efficient asset management involves optimizing how assets are stored and accessed. For large projects, consider using a centralized asset management system where assets are stored in a dedicated repository. This system should allow for easy version control, backup, and retrieval of assets. Utilize software or tools that support asset versioning and tracking to manage updates and revisions effectively.

In Blender, the use of Collections and linking features can help manage large numbers of assets. Collections allow you to group and organize assets within your Blender project, making it easier to manage scenes and assets. Linking features enable you to reuse assets across different projects while maintaining a single source of truth. This means that any updates made to an asset in the source file will be reflected in all projects that use that asset.

Collaborative Asset Sharing: In a collaborative environment, efficient asset sharing is essential. Establish protocols for sharing assets among team members to ensure consistency and avoid conflicts. Use version control systems to manage changes and updates to assets, and maintain clear documentation of asset usage and modifications. Collaboration tools, such as cloud storage and project management software, can facilitate the sharing and tracking of assets in a team setting.

By implementing these strategies, you can create a robust asset management system that enhances your productivity and ensures consistency across projects. Effective asset creation, organization, and integration are fundamental to delivering high-quality animations and models, ultimately contributing to the success of your projects.

Efficient asset management also involves creating systems for updating and maintaining the assets over time. As projects evolve, the need to refine, optimize, or replace assets will arise. To handle these updates smoothly, implement a version control system for your assets. Each version of an asset should be clearly labeled and archived, allowing you to revert to previous versions if needed. This practice ensures that you can track changes, collaborate effectively with team members, and maintain the integrity of your project.

Creating a Robust Asset Pipeline: Establishing a robust asset pipeline is crucial for managing the flow of assets from creation to implementation. This pipeline should include standardized procedures for asset creation, review, and integration. Define clear stages for asset development, such as concept design, modeling, texturing, rigging, and animation. Each stage should have specific criteria and quality checks to ensure consistency and quality across all assets.

Integrate tools and workflows that facilitate collaboration and communication within the team. For instance, using project management software to track asset status, deadlines, and feedback can greatly enhance efficiency. Additionally, implementing version control systems for assets, such as Git or specialized asset management tools, helps manage changes and ensures that everyone is working with the most current version of an asset.

Optimizing Assets for Performance: Asset optimization is essential for ensuring that your projects run smoothly and efficiently. Large, unoptimized assets can lead to performance issues, such as slow rendering times or lag during real-time playback. To optimize assets, focus on reducing polygon counts for models, compressing textures without significant loss of quality, and optimizing animations to ensure they run smoothly in your project.

Blender provides several tools for asset optimization. Use the Decimate Modifier to reduce polygon counts while preserving the essential shape of your models. For textures, consider using efficient image formats such as JPEG or PNG, and adjust the resolution to match the needs of your project. Additionally, leverage Blender's built-in tools for baking textures and lighting information into your assets, which can improve performance and reduce rendering times.

Documentation and Training: Comprehensive documentation and training are vital for ensuring that your asset management practices are effective and sustainable. Document your asset creation and management processes, including naming conventions, version control practices, and integration procedures. This documentation should be accessible to all team members and updated regularly to reflect any changes in practices or tools.

Provide training for new team members on your asset management workflows and tools. Training should cover not only the technical aspects of asset creation and integration but also best practices for maintaining asset quality and consistency. Regularly review and refine your asset management practices based on feedback from the team and lessons learned from past projects.

Leveraging Asset Reusability: One of the key benefits of effective asset management is the ability to reuse assets across multiple projects. By maintaining a well-organized asset library, you can quickly locate and repurpose assets for new projects, saving time and effort. Consider creating reusable asset templates or modular components that can be easily adapted to different contexts.

When repurposing assets, ensure that they fit seamlessly into the new project's requirements. This may involve modifying textures, adjusting materials, or tweaking animations to match the new project's style and functionality. Effective asset reuse not only improves efficiency but also contributes to a cohesive and polished final product.

Collaboration and Feedback: Effective asset management also involves fostering collaboration and incorporating feedback. Encourage team members to provide feedback on assets, whether it's about design, functionality, or integration. This feedback can be invaluable for identifying areas for improvement and ensuring that assets meet the needs of the project.

Implement a system for collecting and addressing feedback on assets. This might include regular review meetings, feedback forms, or collaborative platforms where team members can discuss asset-related issues. Addressing feedback promptly and constructively will help maintain the quality of your assets and ensure that they contribute positively to the overall project.

In conclusion, creating and managing assets efficiently requires a combination of strategic planning, effective tools, and best practices. By building a well-organized asset library, leveraging asset packs, integrating external resources, optimizing performance, and fostering collaboration, you can streamline your workflow and enhance productivity. A focus on documentation, training, and feedback will further ensure that your asset management practices support the successful completion of your projects.

CHAPTER 22: GAME DEVELOPMENT WITH BLENDER

In the realm of game development, Blender serves as a powerful tool for creating and preparing 3D assets that integrate seamlessly with various game engines. This section will guide you through the essential steps of exporting models and animations from Blender to game engines such as Unity and Godot, setting up interactive elements, and preparing your animations for real-time applications. The objective is to bridge the gap between 3D creation and game development, allowing you to leverage Blender's extensive modeling and animation capabilities within an interactive game environment.

To begin, understanding the export process from Blender to a game engine is crucial. Blender supports several file formats that are compatible with game engines, including FBX, OBJ, and glTF. Each of these formats has its own advantages and limitations, making it important to choose the one that best suits your project's needs. FBX is widely used due to its robust support for complex animations and rigging, while OBJ is more straightforward and suitable for static models. glTF is a modern format designed for efficient transmission and loading in web and real-time applications, making it a popular choice for contemporary game development.

When exporting models, ensure that all necessary components

are included, such as textures and materials. Blender's export settings allow you to specify which elements to include and how they should be handled. For instance, when exporting to FBX, you can choose to export only the mesh, or include animations, cameras, and lights. It is essential to review and adjust these settings to ensure that the exported file accurately reflects the intended design of your model.

Animations play a significant role in game development, and Blender's animation tools can be effectively utilized to create dynamic and interactive elements. Exporting animations from Blender involves configuring the export settings to include keyframe data and ensuring that the animations are compatible with the game engine's requirements. For FBX exports, you can select options to bake animations, which ensures that all keyframes are captured and that the animation will play correctly in the game engine.

Once the models and animations are exported, the next step is to import them into the game engine. Unity and Godot both offer user-friendly import processes that integrate Blender assets into their environments. In Unity, you can drag and drop the exported FBX files directly into the project window. Unity automatically generates a prefab for each imported asset, which allows for easy manipulation and instantiation within the game scene. You can then adjust import settings such as scale, mesh compression, and animation options to fine-tune the asset's appearance and behavior in the game.

Similarly, in Godot, importing assets is straightforward. You place the exported files into the project's directory, and Godot will recognize and import them. For complex animations, Godot provides an AnimationPlayer node that allows you to control and play animations within the game. Ensure that your animations are correctly assigned and configured in the AnimationPlayer to achieve the desired effects.

Setting up interactive elements is a critical aspect of game development, and Blender provides tools to create assets that can be used in interactive scenarios. This involves designing models with game functionality in mind, such as collision detection, physics interactions, and user inputs. When creating interactive assets in Blender, consider how they will interact with the game engine's systems. For example, models intended for physics simulations should be designed with appropriate collision shapes and constraints.

Blender's physics simulations, such as rigid body dynamics and cloth simulations, can be used to create assets that interact realistically within the game engine. After simulating these interactions in Blender, you need to ensure that the exported assets are compatible with the game engine's physics system. This may involve simplifying or baking the simulations to ensure smooth performance in real-time applications.

Finally, preparing your animations for real-time applications requires optimization to ensure that they run smoothly within the game engine. This includes optimizing the rigging, reducing polygon counts, and baking animations to minimize computational overhead. Blender's tools for animation optimization, such as the Decimate Modifier and animation baking, can help streamline the process and improve performance in the game engine.

By effectively exporting and importing assets, setting up interactive elements, and optimizing animations, you can leverage Blender's capabilities to enhance your game development workflow. Integrating Blender with game engines opens up a range of possibilities for creating immersive and engaging gaming experiences.

To continue, once the assets are imported into the game engine, the focus shifts to configuring them for use within the game environment. In Unity, this involves setting up materials and shaders to ensure that the assets appear as intended. Unity's material system is versatile, allowing for adjustments to properties such as texture maps, colors, and shaders. After importing, you might need to tweak the materials to match the visual style of your game. For instance, Unity uses its Standard Shader by default, which can be customized for various surface properties like metallicity and smoothness.

In Godot, similar adjustments are required to ensure that your models and animations fit seamlessly into the engine. Godot's material system includes shaders that can be applied and customized through the Shader Language, offering a high degree of control over how surfaces interact with light. Both engines also require you to set up physics properties, which involves assigning colliders and rigidbodies to your models to enable physical interactions within the game world.

Next, attention should turn to the interactive elements that bring your game to life. In Unity, scripting is used to define interactions and behaviors. Unity employs C as its primary scripting language, and it allows you to write scripts that control everything from character movement to complex game mechanics. These scripts are attached to game objects, including the ones you imported from Blender, to define their behavior within the game. For instance, you might write a script to control how a character moves or how an object responds to player input.

Godot uses its scripting language called GDScript, which is designed specifically for game development and integrates closely with the engine's node-based architecture. GDScript allows you to script behaviors and interactions, such as handling player input or defining how objects interact with the environment. Like in Unity, these scripts are attached to nodes within the scene, including imported assets, to define their functionality.

170

Animating characters within the game engine involves integrating the animation data exported from Blender. In Unity, this is managed through the Animator component, which allows you to create and control animation states using Animator Controllers. Animator Controllers manage transitions between different animation states, such as walking, running, or jumping, and can be triggered by various conditions such as user input or game events. The imported animation clips are assigned to these states, and transitions between them are defined through parameters and triggers.

In Godot, animation control is handled through AnimationPlayers and AnimationTrees. The AnimationPlayer node manages animation sequences and their playback, while the AnimationTree node allows for more complex setups, such as blending multiple animations based on certain conditions. You import your animation clips into the AnimationPlayer, set up your animation states, and define the conditions under which animations change.

Both Unity and Godot also support the integration of additional visual effects that can enhance the overall look and feel of your game. In Unity, effects like particle systems, post-processing effects, and lighting adjustments can be added to create more immersive environments. Unity's Particle System allows for the creation of complex effects like explosions, fire, and rain, which can significantly impact the visual appeal of your game. Post-processing effects such as bloom and depth of field can be applied to achieve a cinematic look.

Similarly, Godot offers a range of visual effects through its built-in systems. The VisualShader and ShaderMaterial allow for custom shader effects, while the ParticleSystem node provides tools for creating dynamic particle effects. Godot also supports post-processing effects like screen-space reflections and color correction, which can be used to enhance the visual quality of your game scenes.

Finally, it is crucial to test your assets and animations thoroughly within the game engine to ensure they perform as expected. This includes verifying that animations play correctly, interactions function as intended, and that assets appear and behave as they should in different scenarios. Rigorous testing will help identify any issues or adjustments needed before finalizing your game project.

In conclusion, integrating Blender with game engines such as Unity and Godot involves a detailed process of exporting, importing, and configuring assets. By understanding how to manage these assets and set up interactive elements, you can effectively utilize Blender's capabilities in game development. Whether you're creating dynamic animations, interactive environments, or complex game mechanics, mastering these techniques will enhance your ability to develop engaging and polished game experiences.

To further streamline the process of integrating Blender with game engines, attention must be paid to the export settings and the compatibility of assets. After preparing your models, animations, and textures, the next step is exporting them in a format that your chosen game engine can readily use. Blender supports various formats, but the most commonly used for game development are FBX, OBJ, and GLTF/GLB.

When exporting to FBX, which is a widely supported format for game engines such as Unity and Unreal Engine, it's important to configure the export settings to ensure that all necessary data is included and formatted correctly. Blender's FBX export options allow you to customize what gets exported, such as meshes, animations, and materials. You should verify that the scale is set correctly to match the units used in the game engine. Typically, Blender uses metric units, while many game engines default to centimeters. Adjusting the scale during export ensures that your models appear at the correct size within the game engine.

Moreover, when exporting animations, it is crucial to ensure that keyframes are correctly set and that all animation data is properly baked. This involves converting all animation data into keyframes to ensure that complex animations are preserved correctly in the exported file. Blender's bake animation feature helps with this process by consolidating animation data, which is especially useful for skeletal animations where bones and rigs need to be accurately transferred.

The GLTF/GLB format is another option that is increasingly popular due to its efficient compression and the fact that it is natively supported by many modern game engines. GLTF is designed to be a runtime asset format, meaning it is optimized for quick loading and minimal processing during runtime. This format supports a wide array of features including animations, materials, and textures, and is often preferred for its ease of use and compatibility with web-based applications and real-time engines.

In addition to exporting models and animations, setting up materials and textures for game engines is another crucial aspect. Blender's material settings, such as shaders and textures, need to be adapted for real-time rendering. While Blender uses Cycles or Eevee for rendering, game engines have their own shader systems that may differ from Blender's. It's important to test how these materials appear in the game engine and adjust accordingly. Many game engines have tools or plugins to assist in importing and configuring materials to ensure they match the intended look.

Once your assets are exported and imported into the game engine, you will need to set up interactive elements and test their functionality. In Unity, for instance, you would begin by creating prefabs from your imported models, which allow you to reuse the same asset throughout your game. Unity also provides a robust system for setting up interactions, such as adding colliders, which detect when objects come into contact, and scripts that define how these interactions should behave. In Godot, the process is similar, with nodes being used to define and control the behavior of your assets.

For animating in a game engine, it is crucial to manage animation states and transitions effectively. Both Unity and Godot provide animation systems that allow you to create complex animation states and blend between them smoothly. Unity uses the Animator Controller, which provides a state machine for managing different animation states and transitions. This system allows you to define how and when animations should change based on gameplay events. Godot uses a similar system with its AnimationTree and AnimationPlayer nodes, which help to manage animation blending and transitions.

Testing and optimization are the final steps in the process. It is essential to continuously test how your assets perform within the game engine to ensure they meet the desired quality and performance standards. This includes checking for any issues with textures, ensuring animations play correctly, and verifying that interactive elements function as intended. Profiling tools within the game engine can help identify performance bottlenecks, such as high poly counts or inefficient shaders, allowing you to make necessary adjustments.

In summary, integrating Blender with game engines involves a comprehensive understanding of exporting assets, configuring materials, and setting up interactive elements. By meticulously managing each aspect of the process, from model optimization and animation baking to material adaptation and performance testing, you ensure that your Blender creations translate effectively into engaging, real-time game experiences. The synergy between Blender's powerful modeling tools and the capabilities of modern game engines can result in highly polished and immersive game content, bridging the gap between

3D art creation and interactive game development.

CHAPTER 23:
ADVANCED
TECHNIQUES
AND WORKFLOW
OPTIMIZATION

In the quest for mastering Blender, efficiency and optimization are key to handling complex projects and maximizing productivity. Advanced techniques can significantly streamline your workflow, enabling you to manage intricate tasks with greater ease. This segment will delve into sophisticated strategies and Blender's advanced features to elevate your creative process and improve overall efficiency.

To begin with, mastering the art of customizing Blender's user interface is essential. Blender's flexibility in UI configuration allows you to tailor the workspace to your specific needs, making your workflow more intuitive. Start by creating custom layouts that reflect your project requirements. For instance, if you frequently switch between modeling and sculpting, set up dedicated windows and panels for each task. Utilize Blender's workspace tabs to organize different aspects of your project—such as modeling, shading, and animation—into separate, easily accessible areas. Custom hotkeys and pie menus can further enhance your efficiency. Assigning shortcuts to frequently used tools and commands will minimize the need to navigate through menus, allowing you to focus more on the creative aspects of your work.

Next, delve into the power of Blender's modifiers and non-destructive workflows. Blender's modifiers are crucial for managing complex models and animations. They allow you to apply changes non-destructively, meaning you can modify your model without permanently altering the original mesh. For instance, the Subdivision Surface modifier can smooth out geometry in real-time, while the Boolean modifier can help in creating complex shapes by performing operations such as union, difference, and intersection. By using modifiers, you maintain a high degree of control over your model's final appearance, enabling you to make adjustments without the need for rework.

Another critical technique is the use of Blender's node-based material system. The Shader Editor in Blender utilizes a node-based approach to create and manage materials and textures. This system offers a powerful and flexible way to build complex materials. Begin by familiarizing yourself with the various shader nodes available, such as Principled BSDF, which is a versatile shader node that simulates a wide range of materials. Learn to use texture nodes, mapping nodes, and color correction nodes to fine-tune your materials. Mastering this system not only enhances the realism of your textures but also improves your ability to create unique visual effects.

Additionally, streamlining your rendering process is vital for optimizing workflow. Blender's rendering engines, Cycles and Eevee, each have their own strengths and applications. Cycles, being a ray-tracing renderer, provides high-quality, photorealistic results but can be time-consuming. Eevee, on the other hand, is a real-time renderer that offers faster previews and is well-suited for interactive applications. Understanding when to use each engine is key to managing rendering times effectively. For final renders, use Cycles for its quality and precision, while employing Eevee for quick previews and in-game visuals. Additionally, leverage render layers and compositing nodes to manage and combine different render passes. This technique allows you to separate various elements of your scene, such as shadows, reflections, and ambient occlusion, which can then be adjusted individually in the Compositor to achieve the desired final output.

Moreover, optimizing asset management within Blender is crucial, especially for large projects. Organize your assets using Blender's Asset Browser and Link/Append features to manage and reuse assets efficiently. This is particularly useful for collaborative projects or when working with large libraries of models, textures, and animations. By linking assets rather than appending them, you maintain a single source of truth for each asset, simplifying updates and modifications.

Incorporate custom scripts and add-ons to automate repetitive tasks and enhance your workflow. Blender's Python API allows for extensive customization and automation. You can write custom scripts to handle tasks such as batch processing of files, automatic rigging, or custom export routines. Exploring available add-ons, whether built-in or community-created, can also provide additional functionalities that streamline your work. Many of these tools are designed to simplify complex processes, saving you time and reducing the likelihood of errors.

Lastly, efficiency in project management can be greatly improved by using Blender's built-in features for scene organization. Utilize collections to group and manage objects within your scene, making it easier to control visibility, render settings, and organization. Establishing a clear naming convention for objects, materials, and animations further enhances your ability to navigate complex projects. Good project management practices not only contribute to a more efficient workflow but also help in maintaining clarity and organization as your projects grow in size and complexity.

By integrating these advanced techniques and optimizing your workflow, you can significantly enhance your productivity and effectiveness in Blender. Embracing these strategies will not only streamline your creative process but also allow you to tackle more ambitious projects with greater ease and confidence.

Another cornerstone of optimizing your workflow in Blender lies in efficient project management and organization. As projects become more complex, maintaining an organized structure becomes increasingly crucial. Blender provides several features to help manage large scenes and assets effectively. One such feature is collections, which allow you to group and organize objects within your scene. By categorizing objects into different collections—such as models, lights, cameras, and effects—you can streamline your workflow and improve navigation within the scene. You can also use the Outliner, which displays all the objects in your scene hierarchically, to quickly locate and manage elements.

Linking and appending are additional techniques that can greatly enhance project organization and efficiency. Linking allows you to import objects from other Blender files without duplicating them, which is particularly useful when working on large projects with multiple collaborators. This means that any updates made to the linked objects in the original file are automatically reflected in your current project. On the other hand, appending imports data from another file and creates a copy within your current project. While this method does not maintain a dynamic link, it is useful for creating standalone projects or assets that do not need to be updated dynamically.

For managing complex animations and rigging, Blender's Animation Editors provide powerful tools for refining motion and performance. The Graph Editor allows you to view and edit animation curves, offering precise control over the timing and interpolation of your keyframes. Mastery of the Graph Editor enables you to smooth out animations, correct timing issues, and create more fluid, natural movements. The Dope Sheet complements this by providing a high-level overview of your animation data, including keyframes and action strips. By using the Dope Sheet in conjunction with the Graph Editor, you can streamline the animation workflow and ensure consistency across your project.

Asset libraries in Blender offer another significant advantage for workflow optimization. Blender's asset management system allows you to create libraries of frequently used objects, materials, and presets. These libraries can be accessed and reused across multiple projects, saving you time and effort. You can set up asset libraries by organizing assets into different categories and tagging them for easy retrieval. This approach not only speeds up the creation process but also ensures consistency in your projects by providing a centralized repository of your custom assets.

To further enhance your efficiency, consider leveraging Blender's scripting and automation capabilities. Python scripting in Blender allows you to automate repetitive tasks, create custom tools, and extend Blender's functionality. By writing scripts, you can develop automated workflows for tasks such as batch processing, custom rigging tools, or automated material setups. Python scripts can be executed directly within Blender or saved as add-ons, making it possible to integrate them into your regular workflow. Scripting can significantly reduce the time spent on mundane tasks and increase overall productivity.

Another advanced technique is the use of performance profiling and optimization tools within Blender. As scenes become more complex, performance issues may arise, affecting rendering times and responsiveness. Blender provides built-in tools for performance analysis, such as the Statistics panel and the Performance Profiler. The Statistics panel offers real-time information on the number of vertices, faces, and objects in your scene, helping you identify potential performance bottlenecks. The Performance Profiler, accessible through Blender's preferences, provides detailed insights into memory usage and rendering performance. By using these tools, you can identify and address performance issues, ensuring that your projects run smoothly.

Multi-resolution modeling is another advanced technique that can enhance your workflow. This technique involves creating models at different levels of detail, which can be useful for optimizing performance in real-time applications or games. Blender's Multi-resolution modifier allows you to create and manage multiple levels of detail within a single model. You can sculpt and refine details at higher resolutions while maintaining a lower-resolution base mesh for performance. This approach ensures that your models look detailed when viewed up close but remain efficient when rendered from a distance.

Lastly, embracing version control practices can greatly benefit your project management and workflow. Version control systems, such as Git, allow you to track changes to your project files, collaborate with other artists, and revert to previous versions if necessary. By integrating version control into your Blender workflow, you can maintain a history of your project's development, manage collaborative efforts more effectively, and safeguard against data loss. Blender does not natively support version control, but you can manage Blender files using external version control systems to ensure that your project's evolution is well-documented and controlled.

Through these advanced techniques and workflow optimizations, you can refine your use of Blender, manage complex projects more efficiently, and enhance your overall productivity. By customizing your workspace, utilizing advanced modeling and texturing tools, organizing assets effectively, automating repetitive tasks, and implementing performance optimization strategies, you will be well-equipped to handle the demands of intricate and ambitious projects. These practices not only streamline your creative process but also enable you to produce high-quality work with greater efficiency and precision.

A fundamental aspect of optimizing your Blender workflow involves automating repetitive tasks. Blender's scripting capabilities, particularly with Python, can be leveraged to streamline your process. Python scripting in Blender allows you to create custom tools, automate repetitive tasks, and manage large datasets efficiently. By writing scripts, you can automate processes such as batch renaming objects, setting up scenes with predefined configurations, or even generating complex animations. For instance, a Python script can automate the creation of a series of similar objects with varying parameters, saving significant time when working on projects that require repetitive modeling tasks.

Custom add-ons are another powerful tool for automation. Blender's add-on system supports user-created plugins that extend its functionality. If you find yourself repeatedly performing a set of actions or needing features that aren't natively available, developing or downloading a custom add-on can be a game-changer. There are numerous add-ons available that cater to specific needs, from advanced modeling tools to rendering optimizations. By incorporating these add-ons into your workflow, you can significantly enhance your efficiency and capabilities within Blender.

Performance optimization is also critical, particularly when working on resource-intensive projects. Blender provides several techniques to optimize performance and ensure smooth operation. For example, using proxy objects can help manage complex scenes. Proxies are simplified versions of your high-resolution models, used during the design process to maintain performance. You can switch back to high-resolution versions for final rendering. Additionally, simplifying your scene by reducing the number of visible objects or utilizing Blender's culling techniques can also improve performance. By ensuring that only the necessary objects are processed, you reduce the load on Blender's rendering engine.

When dealing with high-resolution textures and complex shaders, texture management becomes crucial. Efficient texture management involves organizing your textures in a way that minimizes the load on your system while maintaining high visual quality. Consider using texture atlases to combine multiple textures into a single image, which reduces the number of texture swaps during rendering and can improve performance. Blender's texture baking capabilities can also be employed to pre-compute certain aspects of your textures, such as lightmaps or shadow maps, further optimizing runtime performance.

Render settings and optimization play a significant role in refining your workflow. Blender's Cycles and Eevee rendering engines offer different approaches to rendering, each with its own set of optimizations. For Cycles, adjusting the samples setting can significantly impact render times and quality. By balancing the number of samples with your quality requirements, you can achieve efficient renders without sacrificing too much visual fidelity. In Eevee, optimizing settings like screen space reflections and ambient occlusion can enhance performance while still providing high-quality results. It's also beneficial to use render layers and passes to separate different aspects of your scene, such as shadows, reflections, and diffuse lighting. This separation allows for more flexible compositing and can improve render times.

Lastly, effective project documentation and version control can greatly improve your workflow, especially when collaborating with others. Maintaining clear documentation of your project's progress, including decisions made and changes applied, ensures that you and your team can track the development process accurately. Version control systems, such as Git, can be used to manage changes to Blender files and scripts, allowing you to revert to previous versions if necessary and track modifications over time.

By combining these advanced techniques—customizing the user interface, utilizing Blender's modifiers and node-based material system, managing complex projects with collections and asset libraries, automating repetitive tasks with Python scripting, optimizing performance through proxies and texture management, and refining render settings and documentation —you can significantly enhance your productivity and efficiency in Blender. These strategies not only streamline your creative process but also enable you to tackle more complex projects with confidence and ease.

CHAPTER 24: SCENE OPTIMIZATION

Effective scene optimization is essential for achieving smooth performance and efficient resource management in Blender, particularly as the complexity of your projects increases. The optimization process involves several strategies designed to reduce computational overhead, enhance rendering efficiency, and manage memory usage. In this part, we will explore key techniques for reducing polygon counts, optimizing textures, and efficiently managing memory to ensure your scenes perform at their best without compromising on visual quality.

One of the primary aspects of scene optimization is reducing polygon counts. High polygon counts can significantly impact performance, especially when rendering complex scenes. Blender offers several tools and techniques to manage polygon counts effectively. The Decimate Modifier is a useful tool for reducing the number of polygons in your models while retaining their overall shape and appearance. The Decimate Modifier allows you to control the level of detail by specifying a ratio of reduction, ensuring that the visual integrity of your model is preserved as much as possible.

Another technique for managing polygon counts is using level of detail (LOD) models. LOD models are simplified versions of your assets that are used when the camera is further away from the object. By creating multiple versions of your models with varying levels of detail, you can ensure that lower-resolution models are used for distant objects, reducing the computational load during rendering. Blender's LOD management system facilitates this process, allowing you to easily switch between different levels of detail based on the camera's distance from the object.

In addition to reducing polygon counts, optimizing textures is crucial for improving performance. High-resolution textures can consume a significant amount of memory and processing power. To address this, it is important to use texture atlases. A texture atlas combines multiple textures into a single image, reducing the number of texture swaps required during rendering. This approach not only enhances performance but also simplifies texture management within your scene. Blender's UV Mapping tools are instrumental in creating and managing texture atlases. By carefully laying out your UV maps and ensuring efficient use of texture space, you can maximize the effectiveness of your texture atlases.

Texture compression is another effective technique for optimizing texture performance. Blender supports various texture compression formats, such as JPEG and PNG, which can help reduce the file size of your textures without significantly affecting visual quality. When working with textures, it is important to choose the appropriate compression settings to balance quality and performance. For example, JPEG compression is suitable for photographic textures, while PNG is better for textures requiring transparency or higher fidelity. By adjusting compression settings, you can minimize the impact of texture size on memory usage and rendering speed.

Managing memory usage is also a critical aspect of scene optimization. Blender provides several tools to monitor and manage memory consumption, including the Memory Cache Settings and the Statistics Panel. The Memory Cache Settings allow you to configure how Blender handles memory for various operations, such as simulation and rendering. By adjusting these settings, you can optimize memory usage based on the needs of your project. The Statistics Panel provides real-time information about memory usage, including the amount of memory consumed by textures, meshes, and other assets. Regularly monitoring these statistics can help you identify and address potential memory bottlenecks in your scene.

Culling is a technique used to improve performance by excluding objects from rendering that are not visible to the camera. Blender's Frustum Culling automatically performs this task by removing objects outside the camera's view frustum, ensuring that only relevant objects are processed during rendering. Additionally, Occlusion Culling can be employed to exclude objects that are blocked by other objects, further optimizing rendering performance. By effectively utilizing culling techniques, you can reduce the computational load and improve rendering efficiency.

Scene organization also plays a significant role in optimizing performance. Properly organizing your scene by grouping objects into collections and using layers can help manage complexity and improve performance. Collections allow you to categorize and control the visibility of objects within your scene, while layers enable you to isolate and work on specific parts of your project. By maintaining a well-organized scene structure, you can streamline your workflow and reduce the likelihood of performance issues.

Finally, baking is an advanced technique that can significantly enhance performance by pre-computing complex calculations. For example, light baking involves pre-computing lighting information and storing it in lightmaps, which can be applied to your scene during rendering. This approach reduces the computational load during real-time rendering and improves performance. Blender's baking tools, such as the Bake menu in the Render Properties, offer various baking options, including diffuse, specular, and shadow baking. By leveraging baking techniques, you can achieve high-quality results with improved performance.

Managing memory usage is another critical aspect of scene optimization, particularly in complex projects where resource demands are high. Efficient memory management ensures that your scene runs smoothly and reduces the likelihood of crashes or slowdowns. One strategy for managing memory usage involves the careful handling of high-resolution assets. When using high-resolution textures or detailed models, consider their necessity in each context. For objects that are not prominently featured or are far from the camera, lower-resolution alternatives can be used to save memory and improve performance.

Baking is a technique that can help manage memory usage effectively. Baking involves precomputing certain aspects of your scene's data, such as lighting, shadows, or ambient occlusion, and storing these computations in textures. This process reduces the need for real-time calculations during rendering, which can significantly lower memory usage and increase rendering speed. For instance, baking lightmaps can capture the complex interactions of light within a scene, allowing you to render lighting effects without continuously recalculating them.

Another method for optimizing memory usage is using proxy objects. Proxies are simplified representations of more complex models used during the design phase. By replacing high-detail models with lower-resolution proxies while working on a scene, you can reduce the strain on your system's memory. This approach is particularly beneficial when dealing with large-scale environments or scenes with numerous assets. Blender allows you to switch between proxies and full-resolution models easily, ensuring that you can work efficiently without sacrificing the final quality of your renders.

Managing scene complexity is crucial for ensuring optimal performance. Complex scenes with numerous objects, lights, and effects can become unwieldy and impact performance. One effective technique for managing complexity is layering and hiding objects. Blender's Collections system enables you to organize objects into different layers or groups. By hiding or disabling layers that are not currently needed, you can reduce the rendering load and improve responsiveness. This technique allows you to focus on specific parts of your scene without overwhelming your system with unnecessary data.

Instancing is another technique that can help manage scene complexity. Instancing allows you to create multiple copies of an object without duplicating the underlying data, which conserves memory and reduces processing overhead. For example, if your scene contains multiple trees or buildings, using instancing to replicate these objects can significantly reduce the memory footprint compared to creating separate copies of each object. Blender's Particle System and Geometry Nodes are powerful tools for instancing and managing repeated elements within your scenes.

In addition to these techniques, Blender provides various performance monitoring tools that can help you identify and address performance bottlenecks. The Statistics Overlay displays real-time information about your scene's memory usage, polygon count, and other performance metrics. By regularly monitoring these statistics, you can pinpoint areas that may require optimization and make informed decisions about adjustments needed to improve performance.

Render settings also play a significant role in optimizing scene performance. Blender's render engines, such as Cycles and Eevee, offer various settings that can be adjusted to balance quality and performance. For example, in Cycles, you can manage sample rates, noise thresholds, and rendering resolution to control the quality and speed of your renders. Lowering the sample rate or reducing the resolution for test renders can help you achieve faster feedback while working on your scene. Once you're satisfied with the results, you can increase the settings for the final high-quality render.

Blender's simplify options provide additional control over scene complexity during rendering. The Simplify panel allows you to reduce the overall detail of your scene by adjusting settings such as texture sizes, shadow resolutions, and subdivision levels. This feature is particularly useful for maintaining performance during preview renders, enabling you to work efficiently without sacrificing the final quality of your output.

Lastly, file management is an often-overlooked aspect of optimization but is crucial for maintaining a streamlined workflow. Regularly cleaning up your Blender projects by removing unused data, such as orphaned objects or unnecessary assets, can help keep your file size manageable and improve performance. Blender's Data Cleanup tools can assist in identifying and removing unused data, ensuring that your project remains organized and efficient.

In the pursuit of achieving superior performance in Blender, efficient use of lighting and effects is also pivotal. Complex lighting setups and numerous effects can substantially increase rendering times and impact overall scene performance. To manage these elements effectively, one must adopt strategies that balance visual fidelity with computational efficiency.

When working with lighting, consider using simplified lighting models. For instance, instead of relying on numerous complex light sources, you might use fewer lights with broader effects or more efficient light types, such as area lights or point lights, depending on the scene's requirements. Blender provides a variety of light types and settings, each with different performance implications. For example, using baked lighting for static objects can greatly enhance performance. Baking lightmaps, as previously mentioned, involves precomputing light interactions and storing them in textures, which can then be applied to objects. This technique eliminates the need for real-time light calculations during rendering, significantly speeding up the process.

Shadow optimization is another critical consideration. Shadows can add realism to your scenes but can also be computationally expensive. Blender allows you to adjust the shadow quality settings, such as shadow resolution and softness, to balance between visual quality and performance. For instance, using lower-resolution shadows for distant objects or reducing shadow softness can help maintain performance while preserving the overall aesthetic of the scene.

When it comes to post-processing effects, it's essential to use them judiciously. Effects like bloom, depth of field, and motion blur can enhance the visual appeal but also demand additional computational resources. By optimizing post-processing settings, you can achieve the desired visual effects without overburdening your system. For example, adjusting the intensity and radius of bloom effects or the quality of depth of field can help you maintain a balance between visual fidelity and performance. Additionally, applying post-processing effects selectively, only to specific elements or render passes, can help reduce the overall processing load.

Efficient resource management also involves regular cleaning up of your scene. Over time, as you work on your project, unnecessary objects, unused materials, or redundant data can accumulate. Blender provides tools such as the Outliner and Data API to identify and remove these elements. By regularly purging unused data and optimizing your scene's structure, you can reduce memory usage and enhance performance.

Scene optimization is an ongoing process that requires continuous attention and adjustment. As you progress through your project, regularly assess and fine-tune your optimization strategies to address any performance issues that arise. Blender's performance monitoring tools, such as the System

Console and Statistics Panel, can provide valuable insights into memory usage, processing time, and potential bottlenecks. Utilizing these tools allows you to make informed decisions and adjustments, ensuring that your scene remains optimized throughout its development.

Incorporating best practices for scene optimization into your workflow will not only enhance performance but also improve the overall quality of your projects. By carefully managing polygon counts, optimizing textures, handling memory usage efficiently, and balancing lighting and effects, you can achieve high-quality results while maintaining smooth performance. These techniques and strategies will help you navigate the complexities of Blender more effectively, allowing you to focus on your creative vision while ensuring that your projects run efficiently and effectively.

CHAPTER 25: ADVANCED LIGHTING TECHNIQUES

Advanced lighting techniques play a crucial role in elevating the realism and depth of your Blender scenes, moving beyond basic illumination to create more dynamic and visually compelling environments. This section will delve into sophisticated lighting models, including global illumination and high dynamic range (HDR) lighting, and explore the effective use of multiple light sources. We will also examine how to craft mood and atmosphere through nuanced lighting setups, thereby enhancing the visual impact of your animations.

To begin with, understanding and implementing global illumination (GI) is fundamental for creating realistic lighting effects. Global illumination refers to the simulation of how light bounces off surfaces and interacts within a scene, contributing to more natural and convincing lighting. Blender's Cycles renderer incorporates global illumination through techniques such as ray tracing, which calculates the complex interactions of light with surfaces. This approach allows for accurate simulations of indirect light, soft shadows, and light diffusion.

One effective way to utilize global illumination is by setting up environment lighting. Environment lighting, often achieved through HDR images, provides a realistic background illumination that simulates the way light sources in the environment contribute to the scene. HDR (high dynamic range) images are specially designed to capture a wide range of light intensities, from the darkest shadows to the brightest highlights. In Blender, you can use HDR images as environment textures in the World settings to enhance the lighting of your scene, providing a more immersive and realistic ambiance.

Another critical component of advanced lighting is using multiple light sources effectively. While a single light source can be sufficient for basic scenes, complex environments often require a combination of different lights to achieve the desired effect. Consider using a three-point lighting setup, which includes a key light, fill light, and back light. The key light is the primary source of illumination, defining the shape and structure of your subject. The fill light softens shadows created by the key light and adds more detail to the darker areas. The back light, also known as the rim light, helps separate the subject from the background by creating a highlight around the edges.

In addition to the three-point lighting setup, adding additional light sources can further enhance the realism and depth of your scene. For instance, area lights can simulate soft, diffuse lighting and are useful for creating even illumination over a large area. Point lights provide focused light in all directions and are ideal for simulating light sources such as lamps or bulbs. Spotlights can be used to highlight specific areas or objects within the scene, creating dramatic effects and guiding the viewer's attention.

Crafting mood and atmosphere through lighting involves a more nuanced approach. Lighting can profoundly influence the emotional tone and atmosphere of a scene. For example, warm lighting with hues of orange and yellow can create a cozy, inviting atmosphere, while cool lighting with shades of blue and gray can evoke a sense of coldness or melancholy. By adjusting the color temperature and intensity of your lights, you can manipulate the mood of your scene to match the desired emotional impact.

Lighting effects such as caustics and volumetric lighting can add another layer of realism and atmosphere. Caustics simulate the way light is concentrated or scattered when it interacts with transparent materials like glass or water. In Blender, you can achieve caustic effects by configuring your materials and light sources to interact realistically. Volumetric lighting, on the other hand, creates the effect of light scattering through a medium, such as fog or mist. By enabling volumetric effects and adjusting parameters such as density and color, you can enhance the atmosphere of your scene and create visually striking effects.

An advanced technique for controlling light and shadow is using light portals. Light portals are specialized objects that help guide and focus light into specific areas of your scene, improving the quality of indirect illumination. They are particularly useful in scenes with large windows or openings, where they can help simulate natural daylight more accurately. By placing light portals in strategic locations, you can enhance the overall lighting quality and achieve more realistic render results.

Finally, lighting optimization is essential for maintaining performance while using advanced techniques. Complex lighting setups can increase rendering times, so it is important to balance visual quality with computational efficiency. Techniques such as baking lighting, where light interactions are precomputed and stored in textures, can help reduce the rendering load while preserving the desired lighting effects. Additionally, adjusting sample rates and using light probes to gather lighting information from specific areas can further optimize rendering performance.

Mastering these advanced lighting techniques will not only enhance the realism and depth of your scenes but also allow you to create compelling visual narratives through effective lighting design. By understanding and implementing global illumination, HDR lighting, and nuanced lighting setups, you can achieve a higher level of artistic expression and technical precision in your Blender projects.

When it comes to creating mood and atmosphere through advanced lighting setups, it is essential to understand how lighting can influence the emotional tone and visual narrative of your scene. Lighting is not merely about visibility but also about setting the stage for the story you wish to tell. By manipulating various lighting parameters, you can evoke different feelings and atmospheres.

To begin with, consider the color temperature of your lights. The color temperature, measured in Kelvin, affects the warmth or coolness of the light. For a cozy, intimate setting, warm color temperatures (around 2700K to 3000K) can be used to simulate the soft glow of incandescent bulbs. In contrast, cooler color temperatures (above 5000K) can create a more sterile or clinical atmosphere, suitable for scenes set in offices or hospitals. Blender allows you to adjust the color temperature of your light sources through the color settings in the light properties panel.

Another technique to create mood is through lighting direction. The angle from which light falls on a subject can dramatically alter its appearance and the overall scene's atmosphere. Low-angle lighting, for instance, can create long shadows and emphasize textures, which is effective for dramatic or eerie settings. On the other hand, high-angle lighting can produce shorter shadows and a more straightforward, natural look. Experimenting with light direction can help you achieve the desired emotional impact.

Lighting intensity and falloff are also crucial factors. Intensity controls how strong the light source is, while falloff determines how quickly the light diminishes with distance. For scenes requiring subtle illumination, such as a moonlit night, you might use a light source with low intensity and soft falloff to mimic the gentle light of the moon. Conversely, for scenes requiring sharp contrasts and high visibility, such as a spotlight on a stage, higher intensity and a more focused falloff can be used to create stark highlights and deep shadows.

Using lighting layers or render passes can also be highly effective in post-production. By rendering different lighting effects separately, such as direct light, indirect light, and shadows, you gain greater flexibility in compositing. Blender's Render Layers feature allows you to isolate and adjust these different components independently, giving you more control over the final look of your scene. For instance, you can adjust the intensity or color of shadows without altering the main lighting, allowing for finer control over the mood and visual impact.

Incorporating volumetric lighting can add a sense of depth and atmosphere to your scenes. Volumetric lighting, also known as "God rays," simulates the scattering of light through particles in the air, such as dust or fog. This effect can be particularly striking in scenes with light streaming through windows or gaps in structures. Blender's volumetric shaders and settings enable you to control the density and scale of the volumetric effect, helping you create realistic and atmospheric lighting.

Lighting for animation also requires special considerations. Unlike static scenes, animated sequences often involve dynamic lighting setups that must adapt to changes in the scene. For animations, it's important to ensure that your lighting transitions smoothly between frames. Techniques such as keyframe animation of light properties, including intensity, color, and position, can help achieve natural changes in lighting as the scene evolves. Additionally, using light rigs—predefined setups of multiple light sources arranged in specific patterns— can facilitate complex lighting scenarios and ensure consistency throughout the animation.

Finally, when optimizing render settings for lighting, balancing quality and performance is crucial. High-quality lighting effects, such as soft shadows and detailed global illumination, can significantly impact rendering times. By adjusting render settings, such as sample rates and light bounces, you can control the trade-off between visual fidelity and performance. Blender's Adaptive Sampling feature helps manage render quality by increasing sample rates only in areas of the image that require more detail, reducing overall render times while maintaining high-quality results.

Through the thoughtful application of these advanced lighting techniques, you can enhance the depth and realism of your Blender projects, creating compelling visual narratives that resonate with your audience. By mastering the subtleties of lighting, you not only improve the aesthetic quality of your scenes but also gain greater control over the emotional and atmospheric elements that define your work.

To fully exploit advanced lighting techniques, understanding how to leverage volumetric effects is crucial. Volumetric lighting adds depth and atmosphere by simulating the scattering of light through particles in the air, such as dust or fog. In Blender, volumetric effects can be achieved using the Volumetric Scatter Shader. This shader simulates the interaction of light with a medium, creating realistic fog, smoke, or mist.

When applying volumetric effects, it is important to balance their intensity and scale to avoid overcomplicating the scene or causing rendering inefficiencies. The volumetric density should be adjusted according to the scene's requirements. For example, dense fog or smoke might be used for a dramatic effect, while lighter, more subtle effects could enhance realism without overwhelming the viewer. Additionally, the volumetric step size in Blender's render settings can be adjusted to control the precision of the volumetric calculations, impacting both the quality and render time of the effect.

Light probes are another advanced technique used in lighting setups, particularly for capturing and reflecting environmental lighting. Light probes are used to gather light information from the environment, which can then be used to illuminate objects more realistically. Blender supports various types of light probes, such as irradiance volumes and reflection cubes. Irradiance volumes capture the diffuse light information in a scene, which can then be used to simulate complex light interactions. Reflection cubes capture reflective light information, which can be applied to materials to simulate realistic reflections.

In addition to these techniques, advanced shadow techniques are essential for enhancing the realism of your scenes. Shadows can be cast using various methods, each with its own implications for performance and visual quality. Ray-traced shadows provide highly accurate shadow calculations by tracing the path of light rays as they interact with surfaces. While this method produces very realistic shadows, it can be computationally expensive. For less demanding scenarios, shadow maps can be used. Shadow maps involve rendering the scene from the light's perspective to create a depth map that stores shadow information. This method is less accurate but more efficient for real-time applications.

Shadow softness and bias adjustments can further refine shadow quality. Soft shadows, created using techniques like percentage-closer filtering (PCF), mimic the gradual transition from light to shadow, adding realism to the scene. Adjusting shadow bias helps prevent artifacts such as shadow acne or peter-panning, which can occur when shadows appear detached from their cast objects.

Finally, integrating light baking techniques can significantly enhance performance, especially in static scenes. Baking involves precomputing and storing lighting information, which reduces the computational load during rendering. This process can include baking direct and indirect light, shadows, and ambient occlusion. Blender's baking tools allow you to bake various lighting components into textures, which can be applied to objects within your scene. By using baked lighting, you can achieve high-quality results with lower real-time rendering demands, which is particularly useful for game environments or architectural visualizations.

In conclusion, mastering advanced lighting techniques in Blender involves a comprehensive understanding of different lighting models, effects, and their impact on scene performance. By skillfully applying global illumination, HDR lighting, and volumetric effects, you can create scenes with rich depth and atmosphere. Effective use of multiple light sources, shadow techniques, and light baking further contributes to achieving a high level of realism and efficiency. As you continue to experiment and refine these techniques, you will enhance the overall visual quality and impact of your Blender projects.

CHAPTER 26: RENDERING OPTIMIZATION

Rendering is frequently the most resource-intensive phase of the animation process, requiring a significant balance between quality and efficiency. Optimizing rendering settings is essential to achieving this balance, ensuring that render times are minimized while maintaining the desired visual quality. This discussion will focus on optimizing rendering engines, such as Cycles and Eevee, and offer strategies for configuring settings to improve render performance. Additionally, techniques for effectively rendering large scenes and animations will be explored.

When considering rendering optimization, the choice of rendering engine plays a critical role. Blender offers two primary rendering engines: Cycles and Eevee. Each engine has distinct strengths and is suited to different types of projects. Cycles, a path-tracing renderer, excels in producing highly realistic images by simulating the physical properties of light. However, its realism comes at the cost of longer render times due to its computational complexity. On the other hand, Eevee is a real-time renderer that uses rasterization techniques to achieve high-quality visuals with significantly faster render times, making it ideal for projects requiring rapid feedback or real-time applications.

To optimize rendering settings in Cycles, several key parameters should be adjusted. One major factor is sample rates. Cycles uses sampling to approximate how light interacts with surfaces, and increasing the number of samples generally improves quality but also increases render times. To optimize, start with lower sample rates and gradually increase them while checking the render quality. Additionally, use the denoising feature to reduce noise in the rendered image, which can allow for lower sample rates without sacrificing visual fidelity. Blender's built-in denoising options, such as the OptiX and NLM (Non-Local Means) denoisers, help clean up noise effectively while reducing the need for excessive sampling.

Another important aspect of Cycles optimization is render tile size. Tiles are the smaller sections into which the entire image is divided during rendering. Adjusting the tile size can impact render performance significantly. Larger tiles are often more efficient for GPU rendering, while smaller tiles may be better suited for CPU rendering. Finding the optimal tile size for your hardware configuration can lead to considerable improvements in rendering speed.

Adaptive sampling is a technique in Cycles that can further enhance efficiency. This feature allows the renderer to allocate more samples to areas with higher noise and fewer samples to regions with less noise. By focusing computational resources where they are most needed, adaptive sampling helps reduce overall render times while maintaining quality.

In contrast, Eevee relies on approximations and real-time techniques to deliver fast rendering speeds. To optimize rendering in Eevee, you should focus on several key settings. Screen space reflections and ambient occlusion are powerful features in Eevee that add realism but can also impact performance. Adjusting these settings to balance quality and speed is crucial. For instance, reducing the quality or range of screen space reflections can improve render times without severely affecting visual fidelity.

Lighting and shadows in Eevee are another area to optimize. Eevee uses shadow maps and shadow cascades for real-time shadow calculations. Adjusting the shadow map size and the number of cascades can help balance quality and performance. Reducing the shadow map resolution or the number of cascades can speed up rendering, though it might result in less detailed shadows.

Post-processing effects in Eevee, such as bloom and depth of field, should be used judiciously. While these effects enhance the visual appeal of your scene, they can also add to the render time. Adjusting the settings for these effects, such as lowering their intensity or reducing their quality, can help maintain performance while achieving the desired look.

When rendering large scenes, scene management becomes crucial. One technique is rendering in layers or render passes. This approach involves rendering different elements of the scene separately, such as background, foreground, and objects, and then compositing them together in post-production. This method allows for more manageable scene sizes and can make rendering large scenes more efficient. Additionally, level of detail (LOD) techniques can be employed, where lower-detail models are used for distant objects, reducing the overall rendering load.

Scene optimization techniques also contribute to rendering efficiency. For example, reducing the complexity of objects, using simplified shaders, and optimizing textures can all help in rendering large scenes more effectively. Utilizing proxy objects or bounding box modes during the rendering process can also help manage resource consumption and speed up rendering times.

Finally, consider leveraging network rendering or render farms for large-scale projects. These solutions distribute the rendering workload across multiple computers, significantly reducing render times for complex scenes or animations. Blender supports network rendering through its built-in Network Render add-on, allowing you to connect multiple machines to work on a single rendering task.

By carefully adjusting rendering settings, managing scene complexity, and utilizing advanced techniques, you can optimize your rendering workflow to achieve a more efficient balance between quality and performance.

When it comes to optimizing rendering settings in Eevee, the approach differs significantly from Cycles due to the underlying rendering technologies. Eevee, being a real-time renderer, leverages rasterization techniques, which are inherently faster but require different optimization strategies. To achieve optimal performance with Eevee, it's essential to understand and configure several key settings.

First, the render quality in Eevee can be controlled through several options that impact both speed and visual fidelity. One of the primary settings is the sampling rate for both the Render and Viewport. Eevee uses a lower sampling rate compared to Cycles, as it relies on screen space effects and approximations rather than physical light simulations. Adjusting these values allows you to balance between performance and image quality. For real-time applications, keeping the samples lower helps maintain smooth performance, but you can increase them for final renders to enhance detail.

Screen space reflections (SSR) is another critical aspect of Eevee's rendering settings. This feature provides reflections based on the camera's view and can be adjusted for performance. High-resolution reflections add realism but can significantly impact render times. By tweaking the screen space reflections quality and max roughness parameters, you can manage the trade-off between realism and performance. Additionally, using reflection probes can provide better reflection quality without the need for screen space calculations.

Another optimization technique in Eevee involves shadow settings. Eevee supports several shadow techniques, including cube maps and shadow maps. Adjusting the shadow resolution and shadow distance can help control the performance and quality of shadows. Lowering the shadow resolution can speed up rendering times but may reduce the clarity of shadows. Balancing these settings based on your scene's requirements will help achieve a good trade-off between shadow quality and performance.

Ambient occlusion (AO) is also an important feature in Eevee for adding depth and realism to your scenes. AO simulates how light is occluded by nearby objects, enhancing the perception of depth. However, high-quality AO settings can be computationally expensive. To optimize performance, adjust the ambient occlusion distance and intensity settings. Lower distances can speed up rendering while still providing a reasonable approximation of ambient light effects.

When dealing with large scenes, optimization becomes even more crucial. Large scenes often come with increased complexity and higher resource demands. One effective strategy is to use level of detail (LOD) techniques, which involve creating multiple versions of objects with varying levels of detail. This approach ensures that only the necessary level of detail is rendered based on the camera's distance from the object. Blender's Simplify options, found in the Render properties, allow for automatic reduction of detail in distant objects, which can help manage performance without manual LOD creation.

Another technique for handling large scenes is to optimize texture usage. Textures can consume a significant amount of memory and processing power, especially when dealing with high-resolution images. Texture atlases, which combine multiple textures into a single image, can reduce the number of texture lookups and memory usage. Additionally, using compressed textures can lower memory requirements and speed up rendering. Blender provides options to manage texture resolution and compression settings, which can be adjusted based on the performance needs of your scene.

In addition to these strategies, rendering in layers can help manage large scenes and complex animations. By rendering different elements of a scene separately, such as backgrounds, characters, and foreground objects, you can isolate and optimize each layer. This method not only helps with performance but also provides greater flexibility in post-processing. Blender's Compositing Nodes allow for combining and adjusting these layers efficiently, providing control over the final output without needing to re-render the entire scene.

Caching is another valuable technique for handling animations and simulations. Blender's caching systems can store intermediate results of simulations, such as fluid dynamics or particle systems, so that these do not need to be recalculated for every frame. This can greatly reduce rendering times for animations involving complex simulations. The cache settings in Blender allow you to manage how and where these intermediate results are stored, optimizing both performance and memory usage.

Finally, using render farms or distributed rendering can be an effective way to handle particularly demanding rendering tasks. Render farms leverage multiple computers or servers to divide the rendering workload, significantly reducing render times for high-resolution or complex scenes. Blender supports network rendering setups, allowing you to distribute the rendering process across multiple machines, which can be an invaluable resource for large-scale projects.

By implementing these advanced techniques and strategies, you can optimize rendering processes to achieve faster render times and maintain high-quality results. Whether using Cycles or Eevee, understanding and configuring the various settings to fit your project's needs will ensure a more efficient and effective rendering workflow.

When optimizing for large scenes, additional strategies must be employed to manage complexity and ensure that rendering remains efficient. Large scenes, characterized by their high polygon counts, numerous textures, and extensive lighting setups, can significantly impact rendering times and performance. To address these challenges, a combination of techniques should be utilized.

One effective approach is scene instancing, which involves reusing objects or groups of objects within the scene. Rather than duplicating objects, which increases memory usage and computation, you can create instances of a single object. This technique is particularly useful for scenes with repeated elements, such as forests or urban environments. In Blender, this can be achieved through linked duplicates or particle systems that reference the same mesh data, reducing the overall memory footprint and improving render efficiency.

Level of Detail (LOD) techniques can also be advantageous for large scenes. LOD involves creating multiple versions of an object with varying levels of detail and swapping them based on the camera's distance from the object. For example, a highly detailed model can be used when the camera is close, while a lower-resolution version is used for distant views. This reduces the computational load during rendering, as fewer details need to be processed for objects far from the camera. Blender supports LOD through the use of mesh simplification tools and distance-based visibility settings.

Optimizing textures is another crucial aspect of handling large scenes. Large, high-resolution textures can consume significant amounts of memory and processing power. To mitigate this, consider using texture atlases, which combine multiple textures into a single large texture map. This reduces the number of texture swaps required during rendering, thus improving performance. Additionally, ensure that textures are appropriately sized for their usage. For instance, using a 4096x4096 texture for a small object might be unnecessary, and resizing it to 1024x1024 or 512x512 can conserve resources.

Baking is a powerful technique for optimizing rendering in large scenes. Baking involves precomputing certain aspects of the scene, such as lighting, shadows, and global illumination, and storing the results in texture maps. This allows you to reduce the computational burden during rendering by offloading complex calculations. For example, baking ambient occlusion and light maps can significantly speed up render times, as the renderer does not need to compute these effects in real-time.

Effective memory management is also essential for rendering large scenes. Blender provides tools to monitor and manage memory usage, such as the Memory Statistics panel, which displays information about memory consumption for different aspects of the scene. By keeping track of memory usage, you can identify and address potential bottlenecks, such as excessive texture sizes or high polygon counts.

Finally, rendering in layers or passes can improve both performance and flexibility. By rendering different elements of the scene in separate layers or passes, you can isolate and optimize specific components of the scene. For example, you can render the background, foreground, and characters separately and then composite them together in post-production. This approach allows for more efficient rendering and greater control over the final output, as adjustments can be made to individual elements without re-rendering the entire scene.

In summary, optimizing rendering settings requires a nuanced approach that balances quality and performance. By leveraging the strengths of different rendering engines like Cycles and Eevee, employing techniques such as scene instancing, level of detail, texture optimization, and baking, and managing memory and rendering layers effectively, you can enhance both the efficiency and quality of your renders. Each project may present unique challenges, but with these strategies, you can ensure that your rendering process remains manageable and produces high-quality results.

CHAPTER 27:
COMPOSITING BASICS

Compositing is a pivotal phase in the production pipeline where you assemble rendered elements to produce the final image or animation. Mastery of compositing techniques allows you to refine and enhance your renders, integrating multiple layers, applying color corrections, and incorporating various effects to achieve a polished and cohesive result. Blender's node-based compositor offers a powerful and flexible environment for these tasks. Understanding the fundamentals of this compositor will enable you to effectively combine elements, adjust colors, and add finishing touches to your animations.

At the heart of Blender's compositing workflow is the Node Editor, a versatile interface where you can build and manage complex compositing setups. The Node Editor operates on a system of interconnected nodes, each representing a specific operation or effect. Nodes are connected by links that transfer data between them, allowing you to create intricate processing chains. The basic node types include Input Nodes, which bring in various data sources such as rendered images and masks; Filter Nodes, which apply effects and adjustments; and Output Nodes, which render the final composite result.

To start with compositing in Blender, you first need to set up a render layer in your scene. Render layers allow you to separate different elements of your scene into individual passes or layers, such as diffuse, specular, and shadow components. This separation is crucial for effective compositing as it gives you control over each element independently. For example, isolating shadows or reflections can be beneficial for adjusting their intensity or blending them differently in the final composite.

Once your render layers are set up, you can begin assembling your composite. This process starts with adding a Render Layers Node to the Node Editor, which serves as the entry point for your rendered image data. From here, you can use various nodes to process and manipulate the image. One of the essential nodes in compositing is the Color Balance Node, which allows you to adjust the color grading of your image. This node provides controls for changing the overall color temperature, hue, and saturation, which can significantly impact the mood and aesthetic of your final render.

Another crucial aspect of compositing is masking. Masks are used to isolate and protect specific areas of your image during adjustments or effects application. For instance, if you want to apply a blur effect only to the background of your scene while keeping the foreground sharp, you can use a mask to define the boundary between these areas. Blender provides several tools for creating masks, including the Mask Node and the Bezier Mask Node, which allow for precise control over shape and feathering.

Integrating effects into your composite can enhance the visual appeal of your animation. Effects such as glare, blur, and depth of field add realism and stylistic elements to your renders. For instance, the Glare Node can simulate lens flares and light blooms, which are common in high-contrast lighting scenarios. The Blur Node can create a depth-of-field effect by blurring parts of the image based on distance from the camera, mimicking real-world optics.

Color correction is another fundamental aspect of compositing that ensures your final image maintains consistent and accurate colors. Blender's Hue/Saturation/Value Node and RGB Curves Node are powerful tools for adjusting color balance and contrast. The RGB Curves Node allows for fine-tuning color channels and adjusting overall brightness and contrast, while the Hue/Saturation/Value Node provides controls for modifying specific color attributes.

The compositing workflow also involves render passes, which are individual components of a rendered image that are processed separately and then combined in the compositor. Common render passes include diffuse color, specular highlights, shadows, and ambient occlusion. By separating these elements, you can make targeted adjustments to each pass, improving the overall quality of your final render. For example, you might enhance the brightness of the diffuse pass without affecting the shadows, leading to a more balanced and visually appealing result.

Effective compositing also involves rendering out intermediate passes to ensure that you have the flexibility to make adjustments later in the process. This method allows you to revisit and tweak specific elements without re-rendering the entire scene, saving time and computational resources.

Overall, compositing in Blender involves a careful balance of various techniques and tools to create a cohesive and polished final image. By leveraging the Node Editor, mastering color correction, applying effects, and working with render passes, you can transform your raw renders into high-quality animations that meet your creative vision. With practice and experimentation, the compositing process will become a powerful part of your animation workflow, enabling you to achieve professional and visually compelling results.

When working with masks in Blender's compositor, it's important to understand how they can influence the rendering process and final output. Masks allow you to define specific areas of your image for isolated adjustments or effects. This is done through the use of Mask Nodes and Roto Nodes in Blender. The Mask Node is particularly useful for applying corrections or effects to defined areas, such as blurring only the background while keeping the subject sharp. To create a mask, you typically start with a Mask Layer, which can be drawn manually or imported from other sources.

In the compositing workflow, masks can be used in conjunction with nodes like the Blur Node, which applies a Gaussian blur to the areas defined by the mask. This technique is useful for creating depth of field effects or softening backgrounds to draw attention to the focal point of the image. To use a mask with the Blur Node, connect the mask to the node's Mask Input and adjust the blur radius to achieve the desired level of softness.

Another significant aspect of compositing is the integration of effects into your final image. Effects such as glow, lens flares, and color grading can dramatically enhance the visual impact of your animation. Blender provides a range of nodes for these purposes. The Glare Node, for example, can add various types of lens flares and bloom effects to create a sense of light intensity and atmosphere. This node offers different options like Fog Glow, Streaks, and Ghosts, which can be combined to achieve the desired visual effect.

Color grading is an essential part of the compositing process, used to achieve the final look and mood of your animation. Blender's Color Balance Node is a powerful tool for adjusting the tonal values and color balance of your image. This node allows for precise control over shadows, midtones, and highlights, enabling you to correct color casts or achieve specific artistic effects. By adjusting the Lift, Gamma, and Gain parameters, you can fine-tune the color balance to match your artistic vision or correct any discrepancies from the rendered layers.

Combining different layers effectively requires understanding how to blend them seamlessly. Blender's compositor includes several nodes that facilitate this process, such as the Mix Node and Alpha Over Node. The Mix Node allows you to blend two image inputs using different blending modes, similar to those found in image editing software like Photoshop. This node can be configured to use modes such as Multiply, Add, or Overlay, each of which impacts how the layers interact and merge together. The Alpha Over Node is particularly useful for layering images with transparency, enabling you to place one image over another and control the opacity and blend of the top layer.

To create seamless transitions and maintain visual coherence between layers, the Color Correction Nodes are invaluable. Nodes like Hue/Saturation, Brightness/Contrast, and RGB Curves allow you to make fine adjustments to the color and tonal values of your images. For example, using the RGB Curves Node enables you to manipulate the color channels individually, adjusting the contrast and color balance with precision. These adjustments help in achieving a uniform look across various elements and layers in your composition.

In addition to standard compositing tasks, render passes play a crucial role in refining the final output. Render passes separate different elements of the render, such as shadows, reflections, and lighting, into distinct layers. By using these passes, you can make targeted adjustments to specific aspects of your scene without affecting other elements. For instance, if you want to tweak the intensity of reflections without altering the base render, you can use the Reflection Pass to adjust the reflection layer independently. This technique provides greater flexibility and control over the final look of your animation.

Finally, once all the compositing adjustments are made, it's crucial to perform a final review of your composite. Scrutinize your render to ensure that all elements blend harmoniously and that no artifacts or issues are present. Check for consistency in color grading, verify that effects are applied correctly, and ensure that transitions between layers are smooth. This final quality check is essential for achieving a polished and professional result in your animation.

By mastering these compositing techniques, you can significantly enhance the visual quality and impact of your animations. The ability to control every aspect of the final image through node-based workflows, color corrections, and effects integration is key to producing professional-grade animations that effectively communicate your creative vision.

When blending different layers in Blender's compositor, the Mix Node becomes indispensable. This node allows for combining two input images or layers using various blending modes. The Mix Node offers several modes such as Add, Multiply, Screen, and Overlay, each producing different effects depending on the interaction between the input images. For instance, using the Multiply mode darkens the combined image by multiplying the colors of the two layers, which is useful for shadow effects. On the other hand, the Screen mode lightens the image by inverting the colors, making it ideal for simulating light and glowing effects. By experimenting with these blending modes and adjusting their factor settings, you can create complex visual compositions that blend layers harmoniously.

In addition to blending modes, effective compositing often involves adjusting image properties to fine-tune the final output. The Hue/Saturation/Value Node is instrumental in altering the color characteristics of an image. It allows you to adjust the hue, saturation, and brightness of the image, which can help in achieving a specific look or correcting color imbalances. Similarly, the Brightness/Contrast Node provides straightforward adjustments to the image's overall brightness and contrast levels. These nodes, used in combination with others, allow for detailed color grading and enhancement, ensuring that the final image meets your artistic and technical requirements.

Rendering large scenes or animations introduces additional complexities that need careful management. One effective strategy is to use render passes to break down the scene into manageable components. Each pass—such as diffuse, specular, and shadow—represents a different aspect of the rendered image. By isolating these components, you can composite them separately, which not only simplifies the compositing process but also provides greater control over each element's contribution to the final result. The Render Passes Node is key to this approach, allowing you to combine these separate passes into a cohesive final image.

Furthermore, rendering optimizations play a crucial role in managing performance when working with large scenes. Blender's Render Settings offer several options to enhance efficiency. For instance, the Tile Size setting in the Render Properties panel affects how the scene is divided into smaller tiles during rendering. Adjusting the tile size can influence rendering speed, with smaller tiles often improving performance for CPU rendering and larger tiles benefiting GPU rendering. Balancing these settings according to your hardware capabilities can lead to more efficient render times and better resource management.

To address memory and performance issues, you may also consider using proxy objects and simplified versions of high-resolution models. Proxies are lower-resolution versions of objects that allow for faster previews and rendering. By setting up proxy objects in your scene, you can work more efficiently without compromising the final quality of the rendered output. This method is particularly useful for handling complex scenes with numerous high-resolution models or textures.

Post-processing is another important aspect of compositing that involves applying final adjustments and effects to enhance the visual quality. Blender's compositor allows for various post-processing effects, including color grading, vignetting, and film grain. The Lens Distortion Node can be used to simulate optical distortions, adding realism to your scenes. Similarly, the Glare Node, which includes options such as Fog Glow and Streaks, can be used to add realistic light effects that enhance the overall visual appeal.

Ultimately, the goal of compositing is to integrate all the elements of your rendered scenes into a cohesive and visually compelling final product. By leveraging Blender's node-based compositor, you can efficiently combine, adjust, and enhance your layers and effects. Mastering these techniques not only enhances the quality of your work but also streamlines your workflow, allowing for more creative freedom and efficiency in achieving your desired visual outcomes.

CHAPTER 28: ADVANCED COMPOSITING TECHNIQUES

In the realm of advanced compositing, understanding and mastering complex node setups becomes essential for producing sophisticated visual outputs. A crucial aspect of advanced compositing is the ability to create intricate node networks that can manipulate and combine various layers and effects seamlessly. By employing a combination of nodes, you can achieve effects that are both visually compelling and technically precise. One of the primary techniques in this area involves the use of Group Nodes, which allow you to encapsulate complex node setups into a single node. This not only simplifies your node tree but also facilitates the reuse of intricate setups across different projects.

Group Nodes serve as containers for multiple nodes and can be customized with input and output sockets, making them highly versatile for managing complex compositing workflows. When designing a Group Node, it's important to define clear input and output connections, which will allow you to integrate it smoothly into larger compositing trees. For instance, if you have a series of nodes that handle color correction, blending, and special effects, you can group these into a single node for easier management and modification. This method streamlines your workflow and enhances overall efficiency.

Integrating live-action footage with CGI elements is another advanced compositing technique that adds realism and depth to your projects. This process involves matching the lighting, color grading, and motion between the live-action footage and the CGI elements. To achieve this, you will use nodes such as the Alpha Over Node, which enables you to layer CGI elements over the live-action footage. Ensuring that these elements blend seamlessly requires precise adjustments to their transparency, blending modes, and color corrections.

One effective technique for integrating live-action footage is color matching, which involves adjusting the colors of the CGI elements to match those in the live-action shots. The Hue Correct Node and Color Balance Node are instrumental in this process, allowing you to tweak the color balance and tonal values to ensure a consistent look across all elements. Additionally, Match Movie Node can be used to align the color and lighting of CGI elements with live-action footage by analyzing the color profile of the footage and applying corresponding adjustments to the CGI layers.

Another aspect of advanced compositing involves applying visual effects such as lens flares and depth of field to enhance the final output. The Lens Flare Node in Blender's compositor allows you to simulate lens flares and light effects that occur naturally when light interacts with a camera lens. By adjusting parameters such as the flare's intensity, size, and position, you can create realistic and dramatic lighting effects that add visual interest to your animations.

Depth of field effects are crucial for adding realism and focusing attention within a scene. The Defocus Node is used to simulate the blurring of objects based on their distance from the camera, emulating the way real cameras handle focal depth. To use the

Defocus Node effectively, you need to provide a depth map, which indicates the distance of each pixel from the camera. This depth map can be generated from your 3D render or created manually. By combining the Defocus Node with other compositing nodes, such as the Blur Node, you can create a convincing depth of field effect that adds both visual complexity and a sense of focus to your scene.

Managing compositing pipelines for large-scale projects involves coordinating multiple compositing tasks and ensuring consistency across different elements and scenes. This often requires creating modular and flexible compositing setups that can be easily adapted or extended. For example, you might design a modular pipeline where each module handles specific aspects of the compositing process, such as color correction, effects, or transitions. By structuring your compositing pipeline in this manner, you can maintain organization and efficiency even as the complexity of your project increases.

Furthermore, implementing version control and project management practices within your compositing pipeline helps in tracking changes and managing collaborative efforts. Utilizing tools such as Blender's Asset Browser or external project management software can assist in keeping track of different versions of your compositing setups, assets, and rendered elements. This ensures that you can easily revert to previous versions if needed and maintain a clear record of your project's development.

In summary, mastering advanced compositing techniques requires a deep understanding of Blender's node-based workflow, integration of live-action footage with CGI, and the application of complex visual effects. By developing proficiency in these areas, you can enhance the quality and impact of your final renders, streamline your workflow, and effectively manage large-scale compositing projects.

When delving deeper into advanced compositing, mastering

visual effects like lens flares and depth of field can significantly elevate the quality of your final render. The Lens Flare Node, for instance, adds a layer of realism by simulating the optical artifacts produced by bright lights or reflective surfaces within a scene. To use this node effectively, begin by placing it within your node tree where you want the flare to appear. Adjust parameters such as the flare's brightness, size, and color to match the lighting conditions of your scene. It's crucial to consider the source of the light within your composition to ensure that the lens flare complements rather than overpowers other elements.

The Depth of Field effect is another powerful tool for enhancing realism by simulating the camera's focus on certain areas of a scene while blurring others. This effect is particularly useful in guiding the viewer's attention and adding a cinematic quality to your animations. To achieve this, utilize the Defocus Node, which allows you to blur parts of the image based on depth information. You'll first need to render a depth pass, which is a grayscale image indicating the distance of objects from the camera. Connect this depth pass to the Defocus Node to apply varying degrees of blur based on the distance values. Adjusting parameters such as the blur radius and the threshold helps in fine-tuning the effect to achieve a natural look.

For large-scale projects, managing a compositing pipeline efficiently is essential to ensure that the compositing process remains organized and manageable. The pipeline should facilitate the smooth integration of various elements and allow for easy updates and revisions. One approach to managing a compositing pipeline involves creating a Master Node Tree that serves as the central hub for combining and organizing all your composited elements. This master tree should be connected to multiple Sub-Pipelines, each handling specific aspects of the project such as color grading, effects, and compositing passes.

Within this pipeline, establishing a clear naming convention for nodes and layers is crucial for maintaining organization. Each node and layer should be named descriptively to reflect its function and role within the composite. This practice not only helps in navigating the node tree but also facilitates collaboration if multiple artists or teams are involved in the project. Additionally, Version Control systems can be implemented to track changes and manage different iterations of the compositing work, ensuring that you can revert to previous versions if needed.

Another key aspect of managing a compositing pipeline is rendering outputs for different deliverables. In a large project, you might need various versions of the final render, each tailored for different formats or quality levels. Setting up Render Layers and Render Passes allows you to separate different elements of the scene, such as foreground, background, and special effects, into distinct layers or passes. This separation not only streamlines the compositing process but also provides greater flexibility in adjusting individual components without affecting the entire composition.

To further refine your compositing pipeline, consider integrating Automated Scripts that can streamline repetitive tasks and ensure consistency across your project. For example, scripts can be written to automatically adjust node settings, apply standard effects, or generate output files in predefined formats. These scripts can save time and reduce the risk of human error, allowing you to focus more on the creative aspects of compositing.

As you progress in advanced compositing, it becomes increasingly important to maintain a balance between creativity and technical precision. The use of complex node setups, integration of live-action footage, and application of sophisticated visual effects should enhance the overall quality of your work without overwhelming the viewer or detracting from the narrative. Regularly revisiting and refining your compositing techniques will ensure that you are able to deliver visually compelling and technically sound results.

In summary, advanced compositing techniques involve not only the mastery of intricate node configurations and effects but also the effective management of compositing pipelines. By leveraging tools like the Lens Flare Node, Defocus Node, and automated scripts, you can achieve a high level of sophistication in your compositing work. Proper organization, version control, and the strategic application of visual effects will enable you to produce polished and professional final outputs that meet the demands of complex projects.

When managing compositing pipelines for large-scale projects, integrating live-action footage with 3D elements can be particularly complex yet rewarding. The key to a seamless integration lies in matching the lighting, color grading, and perspective between the 3D elements and the live-action footage. Begin by analyzing the live-action footage to understand its lighting conditions, camera angles, and color profile. Use this information to adjust the lighting and shaders in Blender to replicate the live-action environment as closely as possible.

Incorporating camera tracking can further enhance the realism of your compositing. By tracking the motion of the live-action camera, you can ensure that the 3D elements move in sync with the footage, maintaining consistent perspective and scale. Blender's Motion Tracking tools allow you to track specific points in the live-action footage and use this data to create a virtual camera that mimics the real-world camera's movements. Once the camera is tracked, you can import the tracked data into your 3D scene, aligning the virtual camera with the live-action footage.

Color correction is another crucial step in achieving a cohesive look between live-action and 3D elements. Blender's Color Balance node and Hue Correct node provide tools for adjusting the colors of your 3D elements to match the color grading of your live-action footage. Pay attention to the color temperature, saturation, and contrast to ensure that your 3D elements blend seamlessly with the footage. Additionally, using Look-Up Tables (LUTs) can help achieve a consistent color profile throughout your project, especially if you're working with footage that has been graded with a specific LUT.

To handle large-scale projects efficiently, setting up a node group for recurring tasks can save significant time. Node groups are essentially collections of nodes that you use repeatedly within your compositing workflow. For instance, if you have a standard color grading setup or a common visual effect that needs to be applied across multiple shots, encapsulating these nodes into a single node group streamlines the process. You can then easily adjust the settings within the node group, and the changes will propagate to all instances where the node group is used.

Managing render layers and passes is also vital for handling complex scenes. Render layers allow you to separate different elements of your scene into distinct layers, which you can then composite individually. For example, you might render the background, foreground, and 3D elements as separate layers. This separation gives you greater control over each element during the compositing stage, allowing for more precise adjustments and enhancements. You can use render passes to extract specific information from the render, such as shadows, reflections, or ambient occlusion. Combining these passes in the compositor can produce more detailed and polished final results.

Efficient resource management is another consideration when dealing with large-scale projects. As your node trees grow more complex, they can become more resource-intensive. To mitigate performance issues, use proxy rendering to work with lower-resolution versions of your assets during the compositing stage. Once you have finalized the compositing setup, switch back to the high-resolution assets for the final render. This approach speeds up the preview process and reduces the load on your system.

Lastly, establishing a review and feedback loop is crucial for ensuring the quality of your final output. Regularly review your composited shots with stakeholders or team members to gather feedback and make necessary adjustments. Incorporate a structured feedback process where comments and suggestions are documented and tracked. This iterative process helps refine the compositing work and ensures that the final output meets the project's requirements and expectations.

By applying these advanced compositing techniques and maintaining a well-organized pipeline, you can enhance the quality and efficiency of your compositing workflow. Integrating live-action footage with 3D elements, managing complex node setups, and optimizing for performance are essential skills for producing professional-grade animations and visual effects. Mastery of these techniques will enable you to tackle intricate projects with confidence and deliver compelling final outputs.

CHAPTER 29:
MOTION GRAPHICS

Motion graphics, an essential component of modern visual media, involve crafting animated graphical elements that enhance storytelling and communication. In Blender, the creation and animation of motion graphics encompass a range of techniques from text animation to sophisticated graphic transitions and effects. The process begins with understanding the core principles of motion graphics, which include timing, spacing, and the use of visual elements to convey motion and emotion effectively.

The foundation of creating motion graphics in Blender lies in text animation. Text is a versatile element in motion graphics, used for titles, lower thirds, and promotional material. Blender's Text Object allows for extensive customization and animation. Start by adding a Text Object to your scene and entering the desired text. Utilize Blender's text properties to adjust font, size, and spacing. For animating text, the Text Animation tools offer several options. Keyframe animation can be applied to properties like location, rotation, and scale to create dynamic text effects. More advanced techniques involve the use of Modifiers such as the Wave Modifier to add motion or the Displace Modifier to give text a more organic appearance.

Graphic transitions are another critical aspect of motion graphics. These transitions smooth the flow between different visual elements, such as scenes in a video or slides in a presentation. Blender provides a range of tools to create transitions, from simple fades to complex animated effects. To create a fade transition, use the Alpha Over node in the Compositor to gradually blend one graphic element into another. For more intricate transitions, you can animate masks or use the Shape Keys feature to morph graphics smoothly from one form to another. Combining these techniques with Bezier Curves for animation timing can result in fluid, professional-quality transitions.

The integration of visual effects adds another layer of sophistication to motion graphics. Blender's powerful Shader Editor allows for the creation of custom shaders and effects that can enhance the visual appeal of your graphics. For instance, creating a glowing text effect involves adding an Emission Shader to your text material and adjusting its strength. To simulate light interactions, use Glare Nodes in the Compositor, which can produce lens flares and bloom effects. Particle Systems can be employed to create dynamic effects such as sparks or smoke, which can interact with your graphics to add depth and realism.

Animating graphical elements often requires a thorough understanding of keyframes and interpolation methods. In Blender, keyframes are used to define specific points of animation, and interpolation determines how the animation progresses between these keyframes. For smooth, natural movement, use Bezier Interpolation, which allows for easing in and out of animation curves. The Graph Editor is an invaluable tool for refining animation curves, enabling precise control over the speed and flow of animations. By adjusting the handles on the curve, you can create more complex motion patterns and achieve a polished look.

Incorporating camera movements into motion graphics can also add a sense of dynamism and engagement. By animating the camera's position and focal length, you can create cinematic effects that complement your graphical elements. Use Camera

Path animations to move the camera along a predefined path or employ Orbit Controls for smoother, more organic camera movements. Ensure that your camera movements are synchronized with the timing of your graphical animations to maintain coherence and impact.

Lastly, when working on motion graphics for various media, render settings and output formats are critical. Optimize your render settings to balance quality and performance. For motion graphics, consider rendering at a higher frame rate to ensure smooth playback. Blender supports a variety of output formats, including AVI, MP4, and QuickTime, depending on your project's needs. Pay attention to resolution and compression settings to maintain the quality of your animations across different platforms.

In conclusion, mastering motion graphics in Blender requires a combination of creativity, technical skills, and an understanding of animation principles. By leveraging Blender's extensive tools and features, from text animation to visual effects and camera movements, you can create compelling and engaging motion graphics that enhance any visual project.

When delving deeper into the realm of motion graphics within Blender, understanding graphic transitions involves mastering both fundamental and advanced techniques. Beyond simple fades, Blender offers a suite of tools to craft seamless transitions between elements. For instance, creating a slide transition can be achieved by animating the position of graphical elements along the X or Y axis. Utilize the Graph Editor to adjust the interpolation and ease of the transition, ensuring a smooth and natural motion. By adjusting the curve handles, you can fine-tune the acceleration and deceleration of the transition to match the desired visual rhythm.

In more complex scenarios, masking techniques come into play. Masks allow for the creation of intricate transitions where one element appears to reveal or obscure another. To animate masks, start by creating a new Mask Object and drawing the desired shape. Keyframe the mask's properties to animate its influence over time. Using Shape Keys or Vertex Groups in combination with these masks can produce dynamic effects such as a logo peeling away to reveal text beneath. Experimenting with these elements in Blender's Grease Pencil can further enhance your ability to create hand-drawn or stylized transitions.

Visual effects can significantly elevate the quality of motion graphics. Blender's Compositor provides robust tools for integrating various effects into your animations. For instance, applying Lens Flare effects requires adding a Glare Node in the Compositor. Adjust the settings to achieve different types of flares, from subtle blooms to intense starbursts. Combining lens flares with Depth of Field effects enhances realism by simulating the way cameras focus on different points in a scene. In Blender's Camera Properties, adjusting the aperture and focal length can create a realistic blur that draws attention to specific parts of your graphic.

Incorporating particle systems into motion graphics can add dynamic, interactive elements. For instance, if you want to simulate confetti falling from a logo or sparks emanating from a text animation, utilize Blender's Particle System. Configure the particle emitter to adjust properties such as emission rate, particle size, and lifetime. By using the Physics settings, you can control how particles interact with forces such as gravity and wind. For more advanced effects, consider using Particle Fields and Force Fields to influence the movement and behavior of particles within the scene.

Node-based workflows in Blender are central to creating complex motion graphics compositions. The Shader Editor and Compositor both rely on node-based systems that enable intricate layering and blending of effects. To create a visually compelling graphic, combine multiple nodes to adjust color grading, add textures, and integrate effects. For example, a node setup that blends a texture with a color overlay can create unique visual styles. By chaining nodes together, you can experiment with various effects and settings to achieve the desired look.

Managing these elements effectively requires a thorough understanding of compositing pipelines. In large-scale projects, organizing and structuring your node setups becomes crucial for maintaining efficiency and clarity. Use Frame Nodes to group related operations, which helps keep your node tree organized and manageable. Naming nodes and grouping them logically ensures that adjustments and troubleshooting are more straightforward. For collaborative projects, establishing a clear pipeline where each team member understands the node setup and its purpose can prevent errors and streamline production.

Lastly, as you work with Blender's Motion Graphics tools, always consider the final output format and its implications. Render settings should align with the intended use of your graphics, whether for high-definition video or web animations. Pay attention to compression settings and file formats to ensure that the final product maintains its visual quality and integrity. Blender's rendering options, including Output Properties, allow for the customization of resolution, frame rate, and encoding settings, which are essential for delivering a polished, professional result.

To truly harness the power of motion graphics, mastering text animation in Blender is essential. Text animation is not just about making letters move; it's about enhancing the impact of your message through sophisticated visual treatments. Start by exploring the Text Object tools in Blender, which offer a range of customization options. Adjusting font types, sizes, and alignments is fundamental, but the animation capabilities extend far beyond these basics.

To animate text, consider using Shape Keys to manipulate the text's individual properties. By adding shape keys, you can create animations where text characters morph, slide, or even explode into different forms. This can be particularly effective for creating engaging titles or dynamic lower-thirds in your video projects. Another powerful tool is the Text Animation Presets, which provide ready-to-use animation styles such as typewriter effects, bouncing letters, or rotating text. These presets can be customized further to match the specific tone and pace of your animation.

Incorporating graphic effects into your motion graphics enhances visual interest and helps convey your message more effectively. Blender's Shader Editor is a critical tool for creating and applying advanced materials and effects to your graphical elements. For instance, using Emission Shaders can make elements glow or pulse, which is ideal for creating neon effects or highlighting key points in your graphics. You can combine these shaders with Texture Maps to add complexity and depth, giving your graphics a more polished and professional appearance.

The integration of live-action footage into motion graphics requires careful compositing to ensure seamless interaction between the graphical elements and the footage. Utilize Blender's Compositor to layer your animated graphics over live footage. Start by matching the resolution and aspect ratio of your footage with your graphics to avoid inconsistencies. Then, use Alpha Over Nodes to composite your elements, ensuring that transparency and blending modes are correctly applied to create a natural integration. For live-action footage with motion, use Motion Tracking to align animated graphics with the movements within the footage. This involves tracking points of interest in your footage and applying those movements to your graphics, making them appear as though they are part of the original scene.

Creating a compositing pipeline for large-scale projects involves organizing your workflow to handle complexity efficiently.

Begin by structuring your Blender project into distinct stages: pre-compositing, primary compositing, and final compositing. In the pre-compositing phase, separate your graphics into different layers or passes—such as background, foreground, and effects. This segmentation allows for more granular control and easier adjustments. The primary compositing phase involves integrating these layers, where you can use Blender's Node Editor to adjust blending modes, color correction, and other effects. Finally, in the final compositing phase, review and refine the overall look, ensuring that all elements work harmoniously together.

A crucial aspect of managing large-scale compositing projects is maintaining a clear and organized node structure within Blender. Use Frame Nodes to group related nodes together, which helps to manage complex setups and keep your workspace tidy. Labeling nodes clearly and using Reroute Nodes to simplify connections will make your compositing workflow more efficient and less prone to errors.

Additionally, when working on high-resolution projects or animations with significant effects, optimizing performance becomes vital. To handle large data, consider using Proxy Files to lower the resolution of your previews while maintaining the high-resolution output for final renders. Blender's Render Layers feature allows you to render different aspects of your scene separately, such as shadows, reflections, and objects, and then combine them in the compositing stage. This approach not only speeds up rendering times but also gives you greater control over the final image adjustments.

Lastly, testing and iteration are key components of successful compositing. Regularly review your work at various stages of the process to catch and correct issues early. Utilize Blender's Render Preview and Playblast features to test animations and effects before committing to a full render. This iterative approach helps ensure that your final output meets the desired quality standards and effectively communicates your intended message.

By integrating these advanced compositing techniques into your workflow, you can significantly enhance the quality and impact of your motion graphics projects. Whether you're creating dynamic text animations, integrating effects, or compositing complex scenes, Blender offers a comprehensive set of tools to bring your creative vision to life.

CHAPTER 30: CHARACTER ANIMATION

Character animation is a sophisticated art form that requires a deep understanding of both technical and artistic aspects to bring characters to life convincingly. In exploring advanced techniques for character animation, we will delve into the intricacies of animating facial expressions, syncing lip movements with dialogue, and orchestrating dynamic interactions between characters. This process involves an array of tools and principles designed to enhance the expressiveness and realism of animated characters.

At the heart of expressive character animation lies the effective use of shape keys. Shape keys, also known as blend shapes, allow animators to create a range of facial expressions by interpolating between different shapes of a character's face. For instance, to animate a character's smile, you would create a shape key that transforms the character's neutral expression into a smiling one. This is done by sculpting the smile shape on a copy of the character's mesh and then blending it with the neutral shape to create the desired animation. The key to utilizing shape keys effectively is to ensure that the transitions between different expressions are smooth and natural. This requires careful adjustment of the influence of each shape key to avoid any abrupt or unnatural distortions.

Facial rigging is another crucial component of advanced character animation. To enhance the realism and control of facial animations, you need a robust rig that includes not just basic controls but also advanced features like facial bones or control lattices. Facial rigs often involve a combination of bones, shape keys, and control sliders that give animators granular control over facial expressions. For example, a well-designed facial rig might include separate controls for eyebrow raises, lip curls, and eye blinks, all of which can be adjusted independently or in combination to achieve complex expressions. It is also important to set up inverse kinematics (IK) and forward kinematics (FK) for the facial rig, as these systems allow for more intuitive and flexible animation controls.

Lip-syncing is a critical aspect of character animation when your characters speak or sing. Proper lip-syncing ensures that the character's mouth movements match the spoken dialogue, creating a more immersive experience. To achieve this, you must first analyze the phonemes of the spoken dialogue— these are the distinct sounds that make up words. For each phoneme, you create corresponding mouth shapes using shape keys. When animating, you align these shapes with the audio track so that the character's mouth moves in synchronization with the spoken words. Tools such as Blender's Audio Syncing features can help automate some of this process, but manual adjustments are often needed to refine the timing and ensure the lip movements look natural.

Dynamic interactions between characters involve a combination of physical movements and emotional expressions that react to the environment and other characters. This requires a deep understanding of animation principles such as anticipation, overlapping action, and follow-through. Anticipation involves preparing the viewer for an action by showing a smaller, preparatory movement beforehand. For instance, before a character jumps, you might animate a crouch or a preparatory lean. Overlapping action ensures that different parts of the character's body move at different rates, such as a character's hair or clothing continuing to move after the character has stopped. Follow-through involves animating the character's movements to their logical conclusion, ensuring that every action feels complete and natural.

Enhancing character animation with rigging enhancements can also greatly improve the quality and flexibility of your animations. Advanced rigs might include features like dynamic muscle systems, which simulate the natural movement of muscles and skin in response to character movements. These systems add an extra layer of realism by ensuring that the character's skin deforms correctly according to the underlying muscle movements. Additionally, control rigs can be designed with user-friendly interfaces that simplify the animation process, allowing animators to make precise adjustments without needing to manipulate complex bone structures directly.

To further refine your character animation, consider using animation layers and mocap data integration. Animation layers allow you to stack different animations on top of one another, such as adding a secondary animation layer for subtle facial expressions or hand movements on top of a primary body animation. This approach provides flexibility in tweaking and adjusting animations without affecting the underlying layers. Incorporating motion capture (mocap) data can also accelerate the animation process, providing realistic movement data that can be adjusted and refined to fit your character's specific needs.

Mastering character animation involves not only understanding these technical tools but also applying the principles of animation effectively. By combining technical skills with a strong grasp of animation principles, you can create characters that are not only visually stunning but also emotionally engaging and believable.

To achieve accurate lip-syncing, I start by breaking down the spoken dialogue into its constituent phonemes. Each phoneme represents a specific mouth shape that corresponds to a sound in the dialogue. For instance, the "O" sound requires the character's mouth to form a rounded shape, while the "E" sound necessitates a wider, stretched mouth. Once you have identified the phonemes, you need to create a set of shape keys or phoneme-specific facial expressions in your character's rig. These shape keys should be designed to represent the full range of mouth shapes needed for accurate lip-syncing.

Synchronizing these shape keys with the audio can be done through manual animation or by using specialized software tools. Manual animation involves carefully adjusting the shape keys frame by frame to match the timing of the dialogue. This approach, while time-consuming, offers the most precise control over the character's mouth movements. Alternatively, automated tools and plugins can analyze the audio track and generate corresponding shape key animations. These tools can significantly speed up the process but might require additional fine-tuning to ensure the lip movements are perfectly aligned with the audio.

In addition to facial animations and lip-syncing, dynamic interactions between characters are essential for creating realistic and engaging animations. When animating interactions, it is crucial to consider the physical and emotional context of the scene. For instance, if two characters are having a conversation, their body language and proximity should reflect their emotional state and relationship. Characters should move in a way that feels natural in response to each other's actions, maintaining proper spatial relationships and reactive movements. This involves animating physical interactions, such as one character touching another or reacting to a push, as well as emotional responses, such as leaning in during an intimate conversation or stepping back during a moment of conflict.

Principles of animation, such as anticipation, follow-through, and secondary action, play a significant role in creating convincing character animations. Anticipation involves preparing the audience for an action by animating the character's initial movements. For example, before a character jumps, they might bend their knees and crouch. Follow-through refers to the continuation of movement after the primary action is complete. For instance, a character's hair or clothing might continue to move slightly after the character has stopped. Secondary actions add depth to the animation by introducing subtle movements that complement the primary action. For instance, a character's eyes might shift or their fingers might twitch while they are speaking or gesturing. These principles help to create a more natural and fluid animation, making the character's actions feel more realistic and expressive.

Rigging enhancements are also crucial for advanced character animation. Rigging involves creating a digital skeleton for your character, which can be controlled to animate the character's movements. Advanced rigs often include additional features such as facial controls, muscle simulations, and dynamic constraints. Facial controls allow animators to manipulate individual facial features with precision. Muscle simulations can add realistic deformations to the character's body as they move, simulating the effect of muscles and skin interacting. Dynamic constraints help to maintain natural movement by ensuring that parts of the character's body follow physical laws and react appropriately to forces and interactions.

To efficiently manage and streamline the animation process, especially for large projects or complex scenes, it is beneficial to create and manage a compositing pipeline. A compositing pipeline is a structured workflow that integrates different stages of animation production, from initial modeling and rigging to final rendering and compositing. This pipeline helps to organize and manage the various assets and processes involved in creating the final animation. It typically includes stages such as asset creation, animation, simulation, rendering, and compositing. Each stage is linked to the next, allowing for efficient updates and revisions throughout the production process. For example, changes made to a character's rig or animation can be automatically updated in the final render, ensuring consistency and quality across all elements of the animation.

Overall, mastering character animation involves a combination of technical proficiency and artistic sensibility. By refining your skills in shape keys, rigging, lip-syncing, dynamic interactions, and animation principles, you can create more lifelike and engaging characters. Additionally, by implementing a well-organized compositing pipeline, you can ensure that your animation process remains efficient and manageable, even for the most complex projects. With these advanced techniques, you will be equipped to bring your characters to life with greater depth and realism, enhancing the overall quality and impact of your animations.

Incorporating dynamic interactions into character animations requires careful attention to detail, especially when animating interactions between multiple characters. One critical aspect is ensuring that the physical interactions between characters are portrayed realistically. For instance, if one character is pushing another, it's essential to animate the reaction of the second character in response to the force. This reaction should include not just the movement of the character being pushed but also the impact on their facial expressions and body posture. Additionally, animating the interaction's aftermath is crucial; the character might need to regain balance or adjust their stance to reflect the impact of the push.

Emotional states also play a pivotal role in how characters interact. The emotional tone of a scene—whether it's tense, joyous, or sorrowful—should be reflected in the characters' body language and facial expressions. For example, a character showing anger might have a tense posture, clenched fists, and an intense gaze, while a character expressing joy might have relaxed shoulders, an open posture, and a wide smile. Adjusting these emotional nuances can significantly impact the believability and depth of the animation.

When animating facial expressions, it is essential to incorporate a range of subtle changes that reflect the character's internal state. Beyond the primary facial expressions, secondary actions such as slight changes in eyebrow positioning, mouth corners, and eye movements can add realism. For instance, a character who is smiling might also have their eyes slightly squinted, and their eyebrows might be raised just a bit. These small details can make a character's emotions appear more genuine and less mechanical.

Rigging enhancements are another crucial aspect of character animation. Rigging provides the underlying structure of a character model, including bones, joints, and control handles, which facilitate animation. Advanced rigging techniques involve creating more complex rigs that offer greater flexibility and control over the character's movements. For example, incorporating inverse kinematics (IK) and forward kinematics (FK) allows animators to create more natural limb movements. IK is useful for ensuring that a character's feet stay planted correctly while walking, whereas FK allows for more intuitive control over arm movements. Enhancing rigs with additional controls, such as facial rigs or muscle simulations, can further improve the quality and expressiveness of the animation.

Shape keys, also known as blend shapes, are critical for animating detailed facial expressions and nuanced character movements. Shape keys allow you to morph a character's mesh into various expressions by blending different predefined shapes. For example, you can create shape keys for various mouth shapes, eye movements, and eyebrow positions. By combining these shapes in different proportions, you can achieve a wide range of facial expressions. It's essential to ensure that the shape keys blend smoothly to avoid unnatural transitions and maintain the character's facial integrity.

Animation principles such as squash and stretch, timing, and exaggeration can enhance the expressiveness of character animations. Squash and stretch add a sense of weight and flexibility to the character, making movements feel more dynamic. For example, when a character jumps, their body might squash slightly upon landing and stretch when in mid-air. Timing refers to the speed and rhythm of movements, and adjusting the timing can convey different emotions and actions. Exaggeration involves amplifying movements to make them more visually striking and easier to read. For instance, exaggerating a character's reaction to a surprise can make the scene more engaging and expressive.

Lastly, managing animation pipelines is crucial for large-scale projects involving multiple animators and complex scenes. Establishing a clear pipeline involves creating standardized processes for asset creation, animation, and rendering. It's essential to use version control systems to track changes and collaborate effectively. Regular review sessions and feedback loops can help maintain consistency and quality throughout the project. Additionally, integrating tools and scripts that automate repetitive tasks can streamline the workflow and increase efficiency.

By employing these advanced techniques, animators can create more lifelike and engaging characters that resonate with audiences. Each element, from facial expressions and lip-syncing to dynamic interactions and rigging, plays a crucial role in bringing characters to life. With careful attention to detail and a thorough understanding of these concepts, animators can achieve a high level of realism and expressiveness in their work.

Environmental Animation

Animating environments involves not only bringing static scenes to life but also ensuring that dynamic elements such as weather effects, moving objects, and natural phenomena interact convincingly with the characters and the setting. Mastering these techniques is essential for creating immersive and believable scenes that enhance the overall narrative of your animation.

To start, consider weather effects, which are among the most impactful environmental elements. Each weather condition has its own set of characteristics and interactions with the environment. For instance, animating rain requires more than just falling droplets; it involves simulating the effect of rain on surfaces, such as puddles forming on the ground or streaks running down windows. The intensity of the rain, its interaction with light sources, and the impact on the characters' clothing and movement all contribute to creating a convincing rain animation. To achieve this, you can use particle systems in Blender, adjusting parameters like emission rate, velocity, and gravity to simulate different intensities of rain. Additionally, shaders and textures can be used to create the appearance of wet surfaces and reflections.

Snowfall shares similarities with rain but requires its own unique treatment. Snowflakes tend to have a slower, more gentle descent compared to raindrops, and they accumulate over time. You can achieve this effect by using particle systems with low velocity and high particle count to simulate the slow, drifting motion of snowflakes. The accumulation of snow can be animated using shape keys or displacement maps to gradually build up snow on surfaces. Additionally, snow tends to obscure features of the environment, so adjusting visibility and adding slight color shifts can enhance the realism of the snowfall effect.

Wind is another critical environmental factor that influences how objects interact within a scene. Wind affects everything from trees and grass to flags and floating debris. To animate wind effects, you can use Blender's physics simulations, such as cloth simulation for flags or soft body dynamics for trees and leaves. By setting wind forces within these simulations, you can create natural, dynamic movements. For more controlled effects, you might use animated displacement maps or texture coordinates to simulate the bending and swaying of objects in response to wind.

Incorporating natural phenomena like fog, clouds, or lightning can further enhance the realism of an environment. Fog and mist can be simulated using volumetric shaders that add depth and atmosphere to your scenes. Adjusting density and color can create various types of fog, from light mist to dense, enveloping fog. To animate clouds, you can use procedural textures or animated shaders that mimic the movement of cloud formations. If incorporating lightning, you'll need to consider both the visual and audio aspects. Lightning can be simulated with sudden bright flashes and brief, intense light bursts, while the accompanying thunder can be synced with the lightning for a more dramatic effect.

Animating moving objects within an environment requires careful coordination to ensure that they interact believably with their surroundings. For instance, a moving vehicle should leave a trail or displacement in the ground, such as tire marks or disturbed dust. Similarly, objects like floating leaves or drifting debris should follow realistic paths influenced by wind and other environmental factors. Using physics simulations and particle systems can help achieve these effects, while keyframe animation might be employed for more controlled movements.

When animating interactions between characters and the environment, it's important to ensure that these interactions are seamless and realistic. Characters walking through a snowy landscape should show evidence of their footsteps, while their clothing and body should respond naturally to environmental effects such as wind or rain. This involves combining animation techniques with environmental simulations to create a cohesive and immersive experience. For instance, character animations might be adjusted to include slight movements caused by wind or rain, and the environment might be animated to react dynamically to the character's presence.

Another key aspect of environmental animation is the transition of day to night and the corresponding changes in lighting and atmosphere. This transition affects everything from the color of the sky to the shadows cast by objects. To animate this, you can create a time-lapse effect using keyframes to adjust the intensity and color of the light source, simulate the movement of the sun and moon, and modify the environment's ambient lighting. Gradual changes in color temperature and light intensity can simulate the passage of time and enhance the realism of the scene.

Finally, camera movements within an animated environment should be planned to complement the dynamic elements of the scene. Camera paths might need to account for shifting weather conditions, changing lighting, or moving objects. Smooth, cinematic camera movements can help highlight these environmental effects and create a more engaging visual experience.

By mastering these techniques, you can create rich, dynamic environments that breathe life into your animations, making them more engaging and believable.

To further delve into environmental animation, let us explore the intricacies of animating natural phenomena such as fog, clouds, and lightning. These elements play a crucial role in setting the mood and enhancing the realism of your scenes.

Fog and mist add depth and atmosphere, creating a sense of distance and volumetric complexity. To simulate fog in Blender, you can use volumetric shaders. These shaders allow you to create a semi-transparent medium that diffuses light, resulting in the characteristic appearance of fog or mist. You will need to adjust parameters such as density and color to achieve the desired effect. The volumetric scatter node is particularly useful for simulating the way light interacts with the fog, scattering in various directions to create a soft, ethereal look.

In addition to fog, clouds can be animated to enhance the dynamism of your environment. Blender offers several approaches to cloud simulation. For procedural clouds, you can use the built-in clouds texture within the Shader Editor, which can be animated by modifying texture coordinates or color ramps over time. Alternatively, you might employ volumetric clouds for more complex animations. This involves using a combination of noise textures and volumetric shading to create realistic cloud formations that change dynamically. You can animate cloud movement by adjusting the coordinates of the texture and the speed of the cloud motion to simulate different weather patterns, such as drifting cumulus clouds or stormy overcast skies.

Lightning introduces a dramatic, high-energy effect that can significantly impact the mood of your animation. To create lightning, you can use a combination of procedural animation and light flashes. A common technique is to animate the intensity and color of a point light source or a spot light to simulate the brief, intense illumination of a lightning strike. Additionally, incorporating lightning bolts requires the creation of jagged, fast-moving lines, which can be achieved using a combination of path animations and texture animations. A lightning effect can be further enhanced by adding dynamic shadows and flickering lights to simulate the transient nature of lightning.

Transitioning to moving objects within a scene, this aspect includes animating elements such as vehicles, animals, or natural features like flowing water or drifting leaves. Each of these requires specific techniques to ensure realistic movement. For instance, animating a vehicle involves creating a rig that supports movement along a path, with proper adjustments for acceleration, braking, and turning. You can achieve this using path constraints and keyframes to control the vehicle's trajectory and speed. Additionally, the vehicle's suspension and interaction with the ground must be considered, especially if the surface is uneven or interacts with the vehicle's wheels.

Animating flowing water introduces its own set of challenges. Water animations typically involve the use of fluid simulations or displacement maps. Fluid simulations can be used to create realistic moving water by defining the fluid domain and setting appropriate initial conditions. This simulation can be combined with animated shaders to reflect changes in water texture, such as ripples or waves. For less complex scenarios, displacement maps can simulate the appearance of flowing water on a surface, using animated textures to give the illusion of movement without the computational complexity of full fluid simulations.

Leaves, grass, and other plant life also require specific techniques for realistic animation. To animate leaves, consider using particle systems or soft body dynamics to simulate their movement in response to wind. By creating a particle system with leaves as individual particles, you can control their movement and interaction with wind forces. Soft body dynamics offer another approach, allowing leaves to bend and sway naturally based on applied forces. Additionally, using texture animation to simulate leaf movement or changes can enhance the effect.

The interaction between environmental elements and the scene's lighting is crucial. For instance, weather effects like rain or snow will cast reflections and shadows that need to be accounted for to maintain realism. By adjusting the lighting settings to complement the environmental effects, you ensure that shadows and highlights are consistent with the scene's atmosphere. This might involve modifying light intensity, color temperature, or adding additional light sources to simulate the diffuse lighting conditions typical of overcast or rainy weather.

To wrap up the techniques for animating environmental elements, always consider the feedback loop between your animated environment and the characters or objects within it. The environmental effects should seamlessly integrate with the overall scene, ensuring that interactions look natural and contribute to the story's mood. For example, rain impacting a character's clothing should show visible wetness and dripping effects, while moving clouds should cast realistic shadows across the landscape.

By mastering these techniques, you will create environments that are not only visually engaging but also add significant depth and realism to your animations, making them more immersive and compelling.

Continuing with the exploration of animating environments, let's delve into the animation of natural features such as flowing water and drifting leaves. These elements require specific techniques to ensure they interact convincingly with the rest of the scene and add a layer of realism.

Animating flowing water involves creating a realistic simulation of water movement, which can be approached in several ways depending on the complexity required. For basic animations, such as a gentle river or stream, you can use displacement maps to create the appearance of flowing water over a surface. This technique involves mapping a texture that simulates the movement of water and adjusting the UV coordinates over time to animate the flow. For more complex scenarios, such as ocean waves or crashing surf, you might employ Blender's fluid simulation tools. This process involves setting up a domain that defines the space in which the fluid simulation occurs, and then configuring fluid objects to interact with each other within this domain. The fluid simulation settings, such as resolution and viscosity, need to be carefully adjusted to achieve the desired effect, and baking the simulation can take considerable time, so iterative testing is essential.

Drifting leaves and similar lightweight, natural elements can be animated using a combination of particle systems and soft body physics. Particle systems allow you to create a large number of instances, such as leaves or debris, that move according to defined rules. By adjusting the forces affecting the particles, such as wind or gravity, you can simulate the effect of leaves blowing in the wind. For a more detailed approach, you might use soft body dynamics to give individual leaves a realistic, fluttering motion. This technique involves assigning soft body properties to the leaves, allowing them to deform and interact with forces in a natural way.

When animating interactive elements within a scene, such as characters or objects interacting with environmental features, attention must be given to how these interactions affect the environment. For instance, if a character walks through a field of tall grass, the grass should sway and bend realistically as the character moves through it. This can be achieved using cloth simulation or dynamic paint systems, where the grass responds dynamically to the character's movement. Setting up collision detection and ensuring that the environmental elements react appropriately to the character's movements will enhance the realism of the interaction.

To integrate all these elements seamlessly into your scenes, you must consider the overall animation pipeline. This involves planning how each element will be animated, ensuring that interactions between different elements are cohesive, and coordinating the rendering and compositing processes to maintain a consistent look. For complex scenes with multiple animated environmental features, creating a detailed compositing workflow can help manage and integrate various animated layers. This involves using Blender's compositor to combine different render passes, adjust color grading, and apply final effects, ensuring that the final output is cohesive and visually appealing.

Lastly, render optimization becomes critical when dealing with complex environmental animations. Given the computational demands of simulating natural phenomena and interactions, optimizing render settings and utilizing efficient rendering techniques is essential. Techniques such as layered rendering —where different environmental elements are rendered in separate passes and combined in post-production—can help manage rendering times and resource usage. Additionally, employing render farms or cloud-based rendering solutions can expedite the process for large-scale projects.

In summary, animating environments in Blender involves a multifaceted approach, encompassing the simulation of natural phenomena, the animation of moving objects, and the integration of interactive elements. By mastering these techniques and carefully managing the animation pipeline, you can create dynamic, engaging, and realistic environments that enhance the overall quality of your projects.

CHAPTER 32:
EXPORTING AND
FILE MANAGEMENT

Navigating the complexities of exporting and file management is essential for ensuring that your projects are delivered effectively and integrated seamlessly with other software and platforms. Efficient management of files and assets not only enhances workflow but also prevents potential issues during the production pipeline.

The process begins with understanding export options available within Blender, each suited to different needs. For instance, when preparing assets for game engines such as Unity or Unreal Engine, the FBX format is commonly used. FBX is a versatile format that retains detailed information about meshes, textures, and animations, making it ideal for game development. To export in FBX format, navigate to the File menu and select Export > FBX. In the export settings, you can adjust parameters such as the scale of the exported model, the inclusion of animations, and the handling of different object types. It is crucial to ensure that the scale settings match the requirements of the target platform to prevent size discrepancies.

Alternatively, for projects requiring high-quality renders and animations, the Alembic format may be used. Alembic supports complex animations and simulations, making it suitable for high-fidelity visual effects and film production. The export process involves selecting Export > Alembic from the File menu, and configuring settings to include or exclude specific aspects of your scene, such as cameras, lights, or specific mesh types.

When dealing with exporting animations, special attention must be given to how keyframes and action data are handled. Blender's native animation data can be exported in various formats such as BVH for motion capture data or USD (Universal Scene Description) for complex scene descriptions. For animations, the keyframes should be baked to ensure that all movements are accurately represented in the export. This involves selecting the relevant object or armature, then using the Bake Action tool to consolidate all keyframes into a single action before exporting.

File management is equally important, particularly when working on large projects or in collaborative environments. One effective practice is to use a file hierarchy that organizes assets into clear categories, such as models, textures, animations, and scripts. This organization helps in quickly locating specific files and maintaining a clean workspace. In Blender, the use of collections allows for grouping objects in a manner that reflects their function or scene placement, facilitating easier management within the software.

When working with multiple collaborators, maintaining consistent naming conventions is essential. This practice prevents confusion and ensures that files and assets are easily identifiable. Naming conventions should be standardized across the project, with clear identifiers for different asset types and versions. For example, using a prefix to denote asset type (e.g., "CHAR_" for character models or "ENV_" for environment elements) can streamline the workflow.

Handling asset dependencies is another critical aspect of file management. Blender projects often rely on external assets such as textures or reference files. Ensuring that all dependencies are correctly linked or packed into the project is vital for maintaining project integrity. Blender offers the option to pack resources into the .blend file, which consolidates all external references into a single file. This can be done via File > External Data > Pack All into .blend, which embeds all linked assets into the project file. However, for large projects, it may be more practical to manage assets in an external directory and use relative paths to keep the project organized and reduce file size.

For integrating with other software or platforms, it's important to consider compatibility issues. Before exporting, ensure that the target software supports the formats and settings used in your Blender project. When preparing files for integration with software like Adobe After Effects or 3D modeling programs, export formats such as OBJ for static models or EXR for high dynamic range images may be appropriate. It is also beneficial to verify that the exported files retain the necessary data and quality required for your specific use case.

Version control is another essential practice in file management, particularly for larger teams. Implementing a versioning system allows for tracking changes, managing updates, and rolling back to previous states if necessary. Using tools like Git or dedicated asset management systems can help in maintaining an organized workflow and ensuring that all team members are working with the most current version of files.

Lastly, backing up your work regularly is crucial to avoid data loss. Establishing a backup routine that includes saving copies of your project files on different storage media or cloud services can safeguard against potential hardware failures or accidental deletions.

By adhering to these best practices in exporting and file management, you can ensure a streamlined workflow, maintain project integrity, and facilitate smooth integration with other software and platforms. This approach not only enhances the efficiency of your production pipeline but also contributes to the overall success of your projects.

When dealing with asset dependencies, managing linked files and external resources is paramount. Blender projects often rely on a variety of external assets, including textures, sounds, and additional blend files. Ensuring these assets are correctly referenced and packaged with the project avoids issues where files might be missing or paths broken during the export process. One approach to manage dependencies effectively is to use Blender's internal asset management tools. By enabling the option to pack all external data into the Blender file, you ensure that all textures and other resources are embedded within the project file. This feature is accessible via the File menu under External Data > Pack All Into .blend. Packing data ensures that the file is self-contained, reducing the risk of missing assets when the file is transferred or opened on another system.

For collaborative projects, where multiple users may be working on different aspects of the same project, it is crucial to implement a version control system. This involves systematically saving and archiving different iterations of the project file to track changes and prevent data loss. Tools like Git can be adapted for Blender workflows, although it typically requires additional setup to handle large binary files. Blender's built-in functionality, such as incremental saves, can also be employed to keep a history of changes. Using the Save As feature and appending version numbers or dates to filenames helps in maintaining a clear version history.

Another essential aspect of file management is the proper use of file formats for specific purposes. For instance, textures and images are often managed separately from Blender files and exported in formats like PNG or JPEG for 2D images, or EXR for high-dynamic-range images. When exporting textures, the resolution and compression settings should be chosen based on the end-use of the textures. High-resolution textures are crucial for detailed renders, while lower resolutions may be sufficient for real-time applications.

Animation data and rigging information are also critical to handle with care. When exporting animations, especially for game engines or other platforms, ensuring that rigging data is preserved and that the animation curves are correctly interpreted by the target software is crucial. This can be achieved by exporting animation data in formats that maintain keyframe information, such as FBX or Alembic. In cases where specific rigging features or constraints are not supported by the export format, additional adjustments or retargeting may be required in the target application.

Integration with other software or platforms necessitates understanding the compatibility and requirements of the target environment. For instance, if preparing assets for a real-time engine like Unity, you must consider the scale and unit measurements used in Blender, as different engines may have varying default units. Additionally, ensure that materials and shaders are correctly translated or re-created in the target software, as not all rendering engines support Blender's materials directly. For workflows involving visual effects, compositing, or video editing software, exporting in formats like OpenEXR or TIFF can preserve high-quality image data and support complex compositing needs.

Furthermore, effective project organization involves structuring your files and directories to facilitate easy access and modification. This includes establishing a clear folder hierarchy for assets, scenes, and render outputs. Using descriptive names for files and folders helps in maintaining clarity and efficiency throughout the production process. For example, separating folders for raw renders, final outputs, and post-processing assets ensures that each phase of the project is distinctly organized.

In summary, managing the export process and handling project files with precision ensures a smooth and efficient workflow. By utilizing Blender's export tools effectively, organizing assets meticulously, and preparing files with attention to detail, you can avoid common pitfalls and maintain a streamlined pipeline. Whether you are working on a solo project or collaborating with a team, adhering to these best practices for file management and exporting will enhance the overall quality and efficiency of your animation projects.

When addressing the need to prepare files for integration with other software or platforms, several factors must be considered to ensure compatibility and optimal performance. Different platforms and software have specific requirements regarding file formats, data structures, and export settings. For instance, if you are exporting models and animations for use in a game engine such as Unity or Unreal Engine, it is important to understand the preferred file formats and how they handle various data types.

FBX is a widely used format for exporting models and animations due to its compatibility with many game engines and 3D applications. To ensure that FBX exports work seamlessly, you must configure export settings carefully. In Blender, this involves setting the correct axis orientation to match the target engine, adjusting the scale to ensure that models import at the correct size, and choosing the appropriate options for exporting animations, such as including keyframes and rigging data. Blender provides specific settings under the FBX export options that let you control which elements of your scene are included in the export, such as mesh data, materials, and animations. Ensuring these settings align with the requirements of your target platform can prevent issues related to data mismatch or missing elements.

Similarly, for high-quality visual outputs intended for film or rendering applications, Alembic (.abc) can be a preferable format due to its support for complex animations and large datasets. Alembic is known for its ability to handle intricate geometry and animation data efficiently, making it suitable for high-end visual effects and simulations. When exporting to Alembic, careful consideration should be given to options such as exporting the whole scene or selected objects, managing cached simulations, and ensuring that any necessary attributes or metadata are included.

In addition to the technical aspects of file export, managing project files involves establishing a structured file organization system to facilitate ease of access and collaboration. Creating a clear directory structure for your project assets, including separate folders for models, textures, animations, and renders, helps in maintaining an orderly workflow. This organization also aids in troubleshooting and ensures that team members can quickly locate and manage specific elements of the project.

Project backups are another critical aspect of file management. Regularly backing up your work helps to mitigate the risk of data loss due to corruption, accidental deletion, or hardware failure. Automated backup solutions or version-controlled systems can be employed to ensure that multiple iterations of your work are preserved. For instance, setting up a routine to save incremental backups at regular intervals can provide a safety net and facilitate recovery if needed.

Finally, when preparing files for final delivery or integration into other platforms, it is important to perform quality checks to ensure that all elements of the project meet the required standards. This includes verifying that all textures and materials are correctly applied, animations play smoothly, and any interactive elements function as expected. Conducting thorough testing in the target environment, whether it's a game engine, a rendering farm, or another software platform, helps to identify and resolve potential issues before the project is finalized.

By following these practices for exporting and managing project files, you can enhance your workflow efficiency, ensure compatibility with various platforms, and deliver high-quality results. Each step—from handling asset dependencies to organizing files and performing quality checks—plays a crucial role in achieving a successful and smooth production process. Understanding and applying these principles will not only streamline your work but also enhance the overall quality and reliability of your projects.

CHAPTER 33: PROJECT WORKFLOW AND MANAGEMENT

In the realm of animation production, effective workflow and project management are crucial for maintaining productivity and ensuring that the project progresses smoothly from concept to final output. Managing a complex animation project requires a systematic approach to organizing tasks, delegating responsibilities, and ensuring seamless collaboration among team members. This discussion will delve into strategies for managing intricate animation projects, focusing on task delegation, version control, and collaborative techniques, all of which are integral to streamlining workflows and handling large-scale projects efficiently.

A well-structured workflow begins with a clear understanding of the project's scope and objectives. Breaking down the project into manageable tasks is the first step in developing a robust workflow. This process typically involves creating a detailed project plan that outlines each stage of production, from pre-production and asset creation to animation, rendering, and post-production. Establishing milestones and deadlines for each phase helps in tracking progress and ensures that the project remains on schedule.

Task delegation is another critical aspect of project management. In a large-scale animation project, tasks are often distributed among various team members, each specializing in different aspects of the production pipeline. Effective delegation involves assigning tasks based on team members' skills and expertise. For example, while one team member might focus on modeling and texturing, another might be responsible for rigging and animation. Clear communication about responsibilities and expectations helps in avoiding overlap and ensuring that each task is completed efficiently. Tools such as project management software or task tracking systems can facilitate this process by providing a centralized platform for assigning tasks, setting deadlines, and monitoring progress.

Version control is essential for managing changes and updates to project files. As multiple team members work on different components of the project simultaneously, maintaining a system for tracking revisions is crucial. Version control systems, such as Git or Perforce, allow team members to manage and track changes to project files, ensuring that all modifications are recorded and can be reverted if necessary. Implementing a version control system involves establishing a repository for project files and defining a workflow for committing changes, merging updates, and resolving conflicts. This approach helps in maintaining the integrity of project files and prevents issues related to file overwrites or loss of data.

Collaboration techniques play a significant role in ensuring that team members work effectively together. Regular meetings and updates help in aligning the team's efforts and addressing any issues that may arise during production. These meetings provide an opportunity to discuss progress, review work, and make decisions about changes or improvements. Additionally, establishing clear lines of communication through collaboration tools, such as Slack or Microsoft Teams, facilitates real-time discussions and feedback. These tools enable team members to share files, discuss ideas, and resolve issues quickly, contributing to a more cohesive and productive workflow.

Asset management is another critical component of project management. In animation projects, assets such as models, textures, animations, and sounds must be organized and managed efficiently to ensure that they are easily accessible and usable. Implementing a well-structured asset management system involves creating a directory structure that categorizes assets based on type and function, as well as using naming conventions that make it easy to identify and locate files. This system helps in avoiding confusion and ensures that assets are readily available when needed.

Effective project management also involves anticipating and mitigating risks that could impact the project's timeline or quality. This includes identifying potential issues early on, such as technical challenges or resource constraints, and developing strategies to address them. For instance, conducting regular reviews and quality checks throughout the production process can help in identifying problems before they escalate, allowing for timely adjustments and solutions.

Finally, documentation is an often-overlooked but essential aspect of project management. Maintaining thorough documentation of project processes, decisions, and revisions provides valuable reference material for team members and helps in ensuring consistency and continuity throughout the project. This documentation can include design briefs, technical specifications, and workflow guidelines, all of which contribute to a more organized and efficient production process.

In summary, managing an animation project effectively requires a comprehensive approach that encompasses task delegation, version control, collaboration, asset management, risk mitigation, and documentation. By implementing these strategies, you can streamline your workflow, enhance team productivity, and ensure the successful completion of complex animation projects.

When tackling large-scale animation projects, the integration of collaboration techniques is paramount for ensuring seamless communication and effective teamwork. Collaboration goes beyond mere coordination of tasks; it encompasses the synchronization of creative visions and the resolution of technical challenges. Regular team meetings are a fundamental component of this process, serving as a platform for discussing progress, addressing issues, and aligning on objectives. These meetings should be structured to facilitate open dialogue, allowing team members to voice concerns, provide feedback, and share insights.

In addition to meetings, the use of collaborative tools can significantly enhance the efficiency of the workflow. Platforms such as Slack, Microsoft Teams, or project management tools like Trello and Asana provide spaces for real-time communication, file sharing, and task tracking. These tools help in keeping everyone informed about project updates and deadlines, thus reducing the likelihood of misunderstandings or missed tasks. Furthermore, they often include features for setting reminders, assigning tasks, and tracking progress, which are essential for maintaining momentum in a fast-paced production environment.

Another crucial aspect of effective project management is the establishment of clear communication channels. In a collaborative setting, it's vital to define how information will be disseminated and how feedback will be provided. This might involve setting up specific channels or groups for different aspects of the project, such as design, animation, and rendering. Establishing protocols for communication ensures that relevant information reaches the appropriate team members promptly and that feedback is actionable and constructive.

Time management is closely tied to effective project management. Ensuring that each phase of the project is completed on schedule requires careful planning and adherence to deadlines. Implementing a realistic timeline that accounts for potential setbacks and allows for adequate review and revision time is essential. Time management tools and techniques, such as Gantt charts or Kanban boards, can assist in visualizing the project timeline and monitoring progress. These tools help in identifying potential bottlenecks and adjusting schedules as needed to keep the project on track.

Resource management is another critical consideration. Allocating resources efficiently involves managing not only human resources but also technical and financial assets. For instance, ensuring that the necessary software, hardware, and licenses are available and up-to-date is crucial for maintaining productivity. Additionally, budgeting for various stages of the project, including potential contingencies, helps in avoiding financial constraints that could impact the project's progress.

Managing feedback and revisions effectively is integral to the success of an animation project. As the project progresses, feedback from stakeholders or clients may necessitate revisions. Implementing a structured approach for incorporating feedback ensures that changes are handled systematically and do not disrupt the overall workflow. This involves maintaining a clear record of feedback received, prioritizing revisions based on their impact, and coordinating with relevant team members to implement changes.

Finally, documentation plays a vital role in project management. Maintaining comprehensive records of the project's progress, decisions made, and changes implemented provides a valuable reference for future projects and ensures continuity. Documentation should include detailed descriptions of workflows, asset management practices, and any issues encountered along the way. This not only facilitates a smoother transition between project phases but also helps in training new team members and improving overall project management practices.

In conclusion, the effective management of animation projects requires a multifaceted approach that integrates task delegation, version control, collaboration techniques, and time and resource management. By implementing these strategies, you can streamline your workflow, ensure effective teamwork, and manage large-scale projects with greater efficiency and success.

When managing complex animation projects, the implementation of version control is crucial to maintaining the integrity and coherence of the project. Version control systems help track changes to project files, allowing for the preservation of different iterations and facilitating the rollback to previous versions if necessary. Tools such as Git or specialized software like Perforce can be integrated into the workflow to manage changes across different stages of the project. This approach is especially beneficial when multiple team members are working on different aspects of the project simultaneously, as it ensures that everyone is working with the most current and compatible version of files.

Establishing a robust file naming and organization system is essential for effective version control and overall project management. Consistent and descriptive file naming conventions help in easily identifying and retrieving specific assets or versions. For example, including version numbers or dates in file names can prevent confusion and overlap between different iterations of a file. Additionally, organizing files into a structured directory system—such as separating assets, renders, and final outputs into distinct folders—improves efficiency and reduces the time spent searching for specific files.

Another important aspect of project management is the integration of feedback into the workflow. Constructive feedback is vital for refining and enhancing the quality of the animation. Setting up a systematic process for gathering, reviewing, and implementing feedback ensures that revisions are addressed promptly and effectively. This process often involves creating a feedback loop where stakeholders, such as directors or clients, can review work at various stages and provide input. Managing this feedback efficiently requires clear documentation of comments and suggestions, as well as a structured approach for incorporating changes into the project.

Managing deadlines and milestones is a crucial element of workflow and project management. Deadlines ensure that the project stays on track and meets client or production requirements. To manage deadlines effectively, it is important to break the project down into manageable milestones. Each milestone represents a key achievement or deliverable, such as completing a particular scene or rendering a draft. By setting and tracking these milestones, teams can monitor progress and make adjustments as needed to stay on schedule.

Risk management also plays a critical role in project management. Identifying potential risks and developing contingency plans helps in mitigating issues that could impact the project's timeline or quality. For instance, technical difficulties, unforeseen changes in scope, or team member availability can pose risks. Addressing these risks involves creating backup plans, allocating additional resources where necessary, and maintaining open communication with all team members to adapt to any changes quickly.

In conclusion, effective project workflow and management encompass a range of strategies designed to enhance productivity, maintain quality, and ensure the successful completion of animation projects. By implementing task delegation, version control, collaboration techniques, time and resource management, feedback integration, and risk management, teams can navigate the complexities of large-scale projects with greater efficiency and effectiveness. These strategies collectively contribute to a streamlined workflow, allowing animators to focus on creativity and innovation while ensuring that projects are completed on time and to the highest standards.

CHAPTER 34:
FUTURE TRENDS IN
3D ANIMATION

As we look to the future of 3D animation, several emerging trends and technologies are poised to shape the industry in transformative ways. Real-time rendering, AI-driven animation tools, and virtual reality applications are at the forefront of these advancements, promising to redefine how animations are created, experienced, and integrated into various media.

Real-time rendering represents a significant leap forward in animation technology. Traditionally, rendering has been a time-consuming process, often requiring hours or even days to produce a single frame. However, advancements in real-time rendering engines, such as those used in game development, are dramatically reducing these timescales. Engines like Unreal Engine and Unity have pioneered techniques that allow for near-instantaneous rendering of complex scenes, enabling animators to see changes and iterate more quickly. This shift not only enhances productivity but also allows for more interactive and dynamic content creation. By incorporating real-time rendering into animation workflows, creators can achieve higher levels of visual fidelity and responsiveness, making it possible to produce immersive and visually stunning content with greater efficiency.

Another groundbreaking development is the integration of

artificial intelligence (AI) into animation tools. AI-driven technologies are revolutionizing various aspects of animation, from automating routine tasks to enhancing creative processes. For example, AI-powered tools can now assist in generating realistic character movements and expressions based on minimal input, streamlining the animation process and reducing the need for extensive manual keyframing. These tools leverage machine learning algorithms to analyze vast amounts of data and generate realistic animations, allowing animators to focus more on creative direction and less on repetitive technical tasks. Additionally, AI can assist in optimizing workflows by predicting potential issues and suggesting improvements, thereby increasing overall efficiency and creativity.

Virtual reality (VR) is another area where significant advancements are occurring. VR technology is transforming how animators visualize and interact with their creations. Immersive VR environments allow animators to experience their scenes in a fully three-dimensional space, providing a more intuitive and interactive way to refine and perfect their work. This technology also opens up new possibilities for storytelling and viewer engagement, as VR allows for the creation of immersive experiences where viewers can explore and interact with the animation in real-time. The integration of VR into animation production pipelines can lead to more engaging and innovative content, as well as new ways for audiences to experience and connect with animations.

As these technologies evolve, staying current with emerging trends becomes crucial for animators and studios aiming to remain competitive and innovative. Adapting to new tools and techniques requires a commitment to ongoing learning and professional development. Engaging with industry conferences, workshops, and online courses can provide valuable insights into the latest advancements and best practices. Additionally, fostering a culture of experimentation and exploration within creative teams can encourage the adoption of new technologies and techniques, leading to fresh and innovative approaches to animation.

The convergence of real-time rendering, AI-driven tools, and VR represents a broader trend toward increased interactivity and efficiency in animation. These advancements are not only transforming how animations are created but also how they are consumed and experienced. As these technologies continue to develop, they will undoubtedly lead to new opportunities and challenges for animators, requiring them to continuously adapt and innovate.

Looking ahead, it is clear that the future of 3D animation will be marked by rapid technological advancements and evolving industry standards. Embracing these changes and staying informed about emerging trends will be essential for animators and studios seeking to push the boundaries of creativity and production. The ability to leverage new technologies effectively will not only enhance the quality and impact of animations but also open up new possibilities for storytelling and audience engagement.

In conclusion, the landscape of 3D animation is undergoing a profound transformation, driven by advancements in real-time rendering, AI, and VR technologies. These developments are reshaping how animations are created, experienced, and integrated into various media, offering exciting new possibilities for animators and audiences alike. By staying abreast of these trends and embracing new technologies, animators can continue to push the boundaries of their craft and create increasingly engaging and immersive experiences.

The convergence of augmented reality (AR) and 3D animation is poised to create new dimensions in interactive media. AR technology overlays digital content onto the real world, enhancing how users interact with both their physical and digital environments. By integrating 3D animation with AR, creators can produce experiences where animated elements seamlessly blend with real-world settings. This integration allows for innovative applications such as interactive advertising, educational tools, and entertainment experiences that offer a heightened level of immersion. For instance, AR can be used in educational contexts to visualize complex concepts in three dimensions within a real-world environment, providing a more engaging learning experience.

The ongoing advancements in procedural generation also hold significant potential for the future of 3D animation. Procedural generation involves creating complex, algorithm-driven content that adapts to various inputs and conditions, rather than manually crafting every detail. This technique is particularly valuable for generating vast environments, intricate textures, and complex simulations with less manual effort. Procedural methods enable animators to produce expansive and diverse worlds efficiently, which can be especially useful in large-scale projects such as open-world games and virtual environments. The application of procedural generation can lead to richer, more varied content while also reducing the time and resources required to create it.

As we consider the evolving landscape of 3D animation, it is essential to recognize the role of collaborative platforms and cloud-based tools in streamlining production workflows. Cloud technology facilitates real-time collaboration among team members, regardless of their physical location. This capability is particularly beneficial for large projects that involve multiple contributors, such as animation studios and game development teams. By leveraging cloud-based tools, teams can share assets, provide feedback, and make updates in real-time, which enhances efficiency and reduces the risk of miscommunication. Additionally, cloud storage solutions offer scalable options for managing large volumes of data, ensuring that project files are securely stored and easily accessible.

The development of new hardware technologies also plays a crucial role in shaping the future of 3D animation. Advances in graphics processing units (GPUs), for instance, are enabling more complex simulations and higher-quality renderings. Modern GPUs are increasingly powerful and optimized for parallel processing, which accelerates the rendering process and enhances the overall performance of animation software. This progress allows animators to push the boundaries of visual fidelity and realism, creating more detailed and immersive animations. Additionally, innovations in virtual reality (VR) headsets and motion capture systems are providing more precise tools for animators, further enhancing the quality and realism of animated content.

As the field of 3D animation continues to evolve, staying current with emerging trends and technologies is vital for maintaining a competitive edge. Continuous learning and adaptation are key to harnessing the full potential of new tools and techniques. Industry professionals should actively seek out opportunities for professional development, such as attending conferences, participating in workshops, and engaging with online communities. By remaining informed about the latest advancements, animators can integrate cutting-edge technologies into their workflows, resulting in more innovative and impactful animations.

In conclusion, the future of 3D animation is marked by rapid advancements in technology and a growing emphasis on interactivity and immersion. Real-time rendering, AI-driven tools, and VR are transforming how animations are created and experienced, while AR, procedural generation, and cloud-based collaboration offer new possibilities for innovation. Staying abreast of these trends and embracing emerging technologies will enable animators to produce more dynamic, engaging, and realistic content. As the industry continues to evolve, the ability to adapt and leverage new tools and techniques will be crucial for achieving success in the ever-expanding world of 3D animation.

The integration of machine learning and artificial intelligence (AI) into 3D animation processes marks another significant advancement in the field. AI-driven tools are revolutionizing how animations are created and refined by automating repetitive tasks and providing intelligent suggestions for improvements. Machine learning algorithms can analyze vast datasets to identify patterns and generate predictive models, which can be utilized to streamline animation workflows. For instance, AI can assist in automating the rigging process by predicting and applying appropriate joint placements based on the character's geometry and intended movements. Similarly, AI tools can enhance texture creation by synthesizing realistic surface details from a library of reference images, thus reducing the time and effort required for manual texturing.

Furthermore, AI's role extends to enhancing animation quality through techniques such as deep learning-based motion capture. By analyzing and learning from extensive motion capture data, AI systems can generate realistic animations for characters with minimal input from animators. This approach not only accelerates the animation process but also provides a higher level of accuracy and consistency in character movements. AI-driven tools are also improving lip-syncing by automatically generating mouth shapes and facial expressions that match spoken dialogue, which enhances the believability of animated characters.

Virtual reality (VR) is another emerging trend that is reshaping the landscape of 3D animation. VR technology offers an immersive environment where animators can interact with and manipulate 3D models in a fully three-dimensional space. This hands-on approach allows for more intuitive and precise control over animations, as animators can physically move around and view their work from various angles. VR tools also facilitate real-time collaboration, enabling teams to work together within a shared virtual space, regardless of their physical location. This capability is particularly valuable for complex projects that require input from multiple specialists, such as animation, rigging, and visual effects experts.

As VR technology continues to evolve, its integration with animation software is expected to become more seamless. Future developments may include advanced VR interfaces that offer greater precision and ease of use, as well as the incorporation of haptic feedback systems that simulate the sensation of interacting with virtual objects. These advancements will further enhance the creative process, allowing animators to achieve higher levels of detail and realism in their work.

The use of real-time rendering technology is also set to revolutionize the production pipeline in 3D animation. Real-time rendering allows for the immediate visualization of changes made to a scene, significantly speeding up the feedback loop and reducing the time required for rendering final outputs. This capability is particularly beneficial for animation projects that involve complex visual effects or interactive elements, as it enables animators to make adjustments and see results instantly. Real-time rendering engines, such as those used in video games, are increasingly being adopted in animation studios for their ability to deliver high-quality visuals in a fraction of the time compared to traditional rendering methods.

The future of 3D animation will also see the continued development of advanced simulation techniques that enhance the realism of animated scenes. For example, improvements in fluid and cloth simulations will enable more accurate and detailed representations of natural phenomena, such as water flow and fabric movement. These advancements will contribute to the creation of more lifelike and immersive environments, enhancing the overall quality of animated content.

In addition to these technological advancements, staying current with evolving trends in 3D animation will require ongoing education and adaptation. Animators and artists will need to continually update their skills and knowledge to keep pace with new tools and techniques. Engaging with professional communities, attending industry conferences, and exploring educational resources will be essential for staying informed about the latest developments and best practices in the field. By remaining adaptable and open to new technologies, animators can ensure that their work remains innovative and relevant in an ever-changing landscape.

Overall, the future of 3D animation promises to be dynamic and exciting, with continuous advancements in technology driving new possibilities for creative expression. By embracing emerging trends such as AI-driven tools, VR integration, and real-time rendering, animators can push the boundaries of what is possible and create more engaging and immersive experiences for their audiences. The key to success in this evolving field lies in staying informed, adapting to new technologies, and continually exploring innovative approaches to animation.

Made in the USA
Columbia, SC
18 October 2024

44617919R00150